BY THE BOG OF CATS

BY MARINA CARR

★

★

DRAMATISTS
PLAY SERVICE
INC.

for Dermot, William and Daniel

BY THE BOG OF CATS was first produced at the Abbey Theatre, Dublin, Ireland, as part of the Dublin Theatre Festival, on October 7, 1998. It was directed by Patrick Mason; the set design was by Monica Frawley; the lighting design was by Nick Chelton; the stage director was Finola Eustace; and the assistant stage manager was Stephen Dempsey. The cast was as follows:

HESTER SWANE .... Olwen Fouéré
JOSIE KILBRIDE .... Siobhan Cullen/Kerry O'Sullivan
CARTHAGE KILBRIDE .... Conor MacDermottroe
MONICA MURRAY .... Pat Leavy
MRS. KILBRIDE .... Pauline Flanagan
XAVIER CASSIDY .... Tom Hickey
CAROLINE CASSIDY .... Fionnuala Murphy
CATWOMAN .... Joan O'Hara
GHOST FANCIER .... Pat Kinevane
GHOST OF JOSEPH SWANE .... Ronan Leahy
YOUNG DUNNE/WAITER .... Conan Sweeny
FATHER WILLOW .... Eamon Kelly
WAITERS .... Gavin Cleland, Kieran Grimes

CHARACTERS

HESTER SWANE, forty
CARTHAGE KILBRIDE, thirty
JOSIE KILBRIDE, seven, Hester and Carthage's daughter
MRS. KILBRIDE, sixties, Carthage's mother
MONICA MURRAY, sixties, a neighbour
THE CATWOMAN, sixties, lives on the bog
XAVIER CASSIDY, sixties, a big farmer
CAROLINE CASSIDY, twenty, his daughter
THE GHOST FANCIER
THE GHOST OF JOSEPH SWANE, eighteen
YOUNG DUNNE, a waiter
FATHER WILLOW, eighty
TWO OTHER WAITERS

PLACE

Act One takes place in the yard of Hester Swane's house and by the caravan on the Bog of Cats.

Act Two takes place in Xavier Cassidy's house.

Act Three opens in Hester's yard and then reverts to the caravan on the Bog of Cats.

TIME

The present.

Note on accent: Midland. I've given a slight flavour in the text, but the real midland accent is a lot flatter and rougher and more guttural than the written word allows.

BY THE BOG
OF CATS

ACT ONE

Scene 1

*Dawn. On the Bog of Cats. A bleak white landscape of ice
and snow. Music, a lone violin. Hester Swane trails the corpse
of a black swan after her, leaving a trail of blood in the snow.
The Ghost Fancier stands there watching her.*

HESTER. Who are you? Haven't seen you around here before.

GHOST FANCIER. I'm a ghost fancier.

HESTER. A ghost fancier. Never heard tell of the like.

GHOST FANCIER. You never seen ghosts?

HESTER. Not exactly, felt what I thought were things from some
other world betimes, but nothin' I could grab onto and say, that is
a ghost.

GHOST FANCIER. Well, where there's ghosts there's ghost
fanciers.

HESTER. That so? So what do you do, Mr. Ghost Fancier? Eye
up ghosts? Have love affairs with them?

GHOST FANCIER. Dependin' on the ghost. I've trailed you a
while. What're you doin' draggin' the corpse of a swan behind ya
like it was your shadow?

HESTER. This is auld Black Wing. I've known her the longest
time. We used play together when I was a young wan. Wance I had
to lave the Bog of Cats and when I returned years later this swan
here came swoopin' over the bog to welcome me home, came right

7

up to me and kissed me hand. Found her frozen in a bog hole last night, had to rip her from the ice, left half her underbelly.

GHOST FANCIER. No one ever tell ya it's dangerous to interfere with swans, especially black wans?

HESTER. Only an auld superstition to keep people afraid. I only want to bury her. I can't be struck down for that, can I?

GHOST FANCIER. You live in that caravan over there?

HESTER. Used to; live up the lane now. In a house, though I've never felt at home in it. But you, Mr. Ghost Fancier, what ghost are you ghoulin' for around here?

GHOST FANCIER. I'm ghoulin' for a woman be the name of Hester Swane.

HESTER. I'm Hester Swane.

GHOST FANCIER. You couldn't be, you're alive.

HESTER. I certainly am and aim to stay that way.

GHOST FANCIER. *(Looks around, confused.)* Is it sunrise or sunset?

HESTER. Why do ya want to know?

GHOST FANCIER. Just tell me.

HESTER. It's that hour when it could be aither dawn or dusk, the light bein' so similar. But it's dawn, see there's the sun comin' up.

GHOST FANCIER. Then I'm too previous. I mistook this hour for dusk. A thousand apologies. *(Goes to exit, Hester stops him.)*

HESTER. What do ya mean you're too previous? Who are ya? Really?

GHOST FANCIER. I'm sorry for intrudin' upon you like this. It's not usually my style. *(Lifts his hat, walks off.)*

HESTER. *(Shouts after him.)* Come back! — I can't die — I have a daughter. *(Monica enters.)*

MONICA. What's wrong of ya, Hester? What are ya shoutin' at?

HESTER. Don't ya see him?

MONICA. Who?

HESTER. Him!

MONICA. I don't see anywan.

HESTER. Over there. *(Points.)*

MONICA. There's no wan, but ya know this auld bog, always shiftin' and changin' and coddin' the eye. What's that you've there? Oh, Black Wing, what happened to her?

HESTER. Auld age, I'll wager, found her frozed last night.

MONICA. *(Touches the swan's wing.)* Well, she'd good innin's, way past the life span of swans. Ya look half frozed yourself, walkin' all night again, were ya? Ya'll cetch your death in this weather. Five below the forecast said and worser promised.

HESTER. Swear the age of ice have returned. Wouldn't ya almost wish if it had, do away with us all like the dinosaurs.

MONICA. I would not indeed — are you lavin' or what, Hester?

HESTER. Don't keep axin' me that.

MONICA. Ya know you're welcome in my little shack.

HESTER. I'm goin' nowhere. This here is my house and my garden and my stretch of the bog and no wan's runnin' me out of here.

MONICA. I came up to see if ya wanted me to take Josie down for her breakfast.

HESTER. She's still asleep.

MONICA. The child, Hester, ya have to pull yourself together for her, you're goin' to have to stop this broodin', put your life back together again.

HESTER. Wasn't me as pulled it asunder.

MONICA. And you're goin' to have to lave this house, isn't yours anymore. Down in Daly's doin' me shoppin' and Caroline Cassidy there talkin' about how she was goin' to mow this place to the ground and build a new house from scratch.

HESTER. Caroline Cassidy. I'll sourt her out. It's not her is the problem anyway, she's just wan of the smaller details.

MONICA. Well, you've left it late for dealin' with her for she has her heart set on everythin' that's yours.

HESTER. If he thinks he can go on treatin' me the way he's been treatin' me, he's another thing comin'. I'm not to be flung aside at his biddin'. He'd be nothin' today if it wasn't for me.

MONICA. Sure the whole parish knows that.

HESTER. Well, if they do, why're yees all just standin' back and gawkin'. Think yees all Hester Swane with her tinker blood is gettin' no more than she deserves. Think yees all she's too many notions, built her life up from a caravan on the side of the bog. Think yees all she's taken a step above herself in gettin' Carthage Kilbride into her bed. Think yees all yees knew it'd never last. Well, yees are thinkin' wrong. Carthage Kilbride is mine for always or until I say he is no longer mine. I'm the one who chooses and discards, not him, and certainly not any of yees. And I'm not runnin' with me tail between me legs just because certain people wants me out of their way.

MONICA. You're angry now and not thinkin' straight.

HESTER. If he'd only come back, we'd be alright, if I could just have him for a few days on me own with no wan stickin' their nose in.

MONICA. Hester, he's gone from ya and he's not comin' back.

HESTER. Ah you think ya know everythin' about me and Carthage. Well, ya don't. There's things about me and Carthage no wan knows except the two of us. And I'm not talkin' about love. Love is for fools and children. Our bond is harder, like two rocks we are, grindin' off of wan another and maybe all the closer for that.

MONICA. That's all in your own head, the man cares nothin' for ya, else why would he go on the way he does.

HESTER. My life doesn't hang together without him.

MONICA. You're talkin' riddles now.

HESTER. Carthage knows what I'm talkin' about — I suppose I may bury auld Black Wing before Josie wakes and sees her. (*Begins walking off.*)

MONICA. I'll come up to see ya in a while, bring yees up some lunch, help ya pack.

HESTER. There'll be no packin' done around here. (*And exit both in opposite directions.*)

Scene 2

The sound of a child's voice comes from the house. She enters after a while, Josie Kilbride, seven, barefoot, pyjamas, kicking the snow, singing.

JOSIE.
By the Bog of Cats I dreamed a dream of wooing.
I heard your clear voice to me a-calling
That I must go though it be my undoing.

10

By the Bog of Cats I'll stay no more a-rueing —
Mam — Mam — *(Continues playing in the snow, singing.)*
   To the Bog of Cats I one day will return,
   In mortal form or in ghostly form,
   And I will find you there and there with you sojourn,
   Forever by the Bog of Cats, my darling one.
(Mrs. Kilbride has entered, togged up against the biting cold, a shawl over her face.)
MRS. K. Well, good mornin', ya little wagon of a girl child.
JOSIE. Mornin' yourself, y'auld wagon of a Granny witch.
MRS. K. I tould ya not to call me Granny.
JOSIE. Grandmother — Did ya see me Mam, did ya?
MRS. K. Aye, seen her whooshin' by on her broom half an hour back.
JOSIE. Did yees crash?
MRS. K. Get in, ya pup, and put on some clothes before Jack Frost ates your toes for breakfast. Get in till I dress ya.
JOSIE. I know how to dress meself.
MRS. K. Then dress yourself and stop braggin' about it. Get in. Get in. *(And exit the pair to the house.)*

Scene 3

Enter Hester by the caravan. She digs a grave for the swan. Enter the Catwoman, a woman in her late fifties, stained a streaky brown from the bog, a coat of cat fur that reaches to the ground, studded with cat's eyes and cat paws. She is blind and carries a stick.

CATWOMAN. What're ya doin' there?
HESTER. None of your business now, Catwoman.
CATWOMAN. You're buryin' auld Black Wing, aren't ya?
HESTER. How d'ya know?
CATWOMAN. I know everythin' that happens on this bog. I'm

11

the Keeper of the Bog of Cats in case ya forgotten? I own this bog.

HESTER. Ya own nothin', Catwoman, except your little house of turf and your hundred odd mousetraps and anythin' ya can rob and I'm missin' a garden chair so ya better bring it back.

CATWOMAN. I only took it because ya won't be needin' it anymore.

HESTER. Won't I? If ya don't bring it back I'll have to go down meself and maybe knock your little turf house down.

CATWOMAN. You just dare.

HESTER. I'll bring down diesel, burn ya out.

CATWOMAN. Alright! Alright! I'll bring back your garden chair, fierce uncomfortable anyway, not wan of the cats'd sleep on it. Here, give her to me a minute, auld Black Wing. *(Hester does.)* She came to my door last night and tapped on it as she often did, only last night she wouldn't come in. I bent down and she puts her wing on me cheek and I knew this was farewell. Then I heard her tired auld wingbeat, shaky and off kilter and then the thud of her fallin' out of the sky onto the ice. She must've died on the wing or soon after. *(Kisses the black swan.)* Goodbye, auld thing, and safe journey. Here, put her in the ground. *(Hester does and begins shovelling in clay. Catwoman stands there leaning on her stick, produces a mouse from her pocket.)* A saucer of milk there, Hester Swane.

HESTER. I've no milk here today. You may go up to the house for your saucer of milk and, I told ya, I don't want ya pawin' mice around me, dirty auld yokes, full of diseases.

CATWOMAN. And you aren't, you clean as the snow, Hester Swane?

HESTER. Did I say I was?

CATWOMAN. I knew your mother, I helped her bring ya into the world, knew ya when ya were chained like a rabied pup to this auld caravan, so don't you look down on me for handlin' a mouse or two.

HESTER. If ya could just see yourself and the mouse fur growin' out of your teeth. Disgustin'.

CATWOMAN. I need mice the way you need whiskey.

HESTER. Ah, go on and lave me alone, Catwoman, I'm in no mood for ya today.

CATWOMAN. Bet ya aren't. I had a dream about ya last night.

HESTER. Spare me your visions and dreams, enough of me own to deal with.

CATWOMAN. Dreamt ya were a black train motorin' through the Bog of Cats and, oh, the scorch off of this train and it blastin' by and all the bog was dark in your wake, ya even quinched the jack-a'-lantern and I had to run from the burn. Hester Swane, you'll bring this place down by evenin'.

HESTER. I know.

CATWOMAN. Do ya now? Then why don't ya lave? If ya lave this place you'll be alright. That's what I came by to tell ya.

HESTER. Ah, how can I lave the Bog of Cats, everythin' I'm connected to is here. I'd rather die.

CATWOMAN. Then die ya will.

HESTER. There's sympathy for ya! That's just what I need to hear.

CATWOMAN. Ya want sugar plum platitudes, go talk to Monica Murray or anyone else around here. You're my match in witchery, Hester, same as your mother was, it may even be ya surpass us both and the way ya go on as if God only gave ya a little frog of a brain instead of the gift of seein' things as they are, not as they should be, but exactly as they are. Ya know what I think?

HESTER. What?

CATWOMAN. I been thinkin' a while now that there's some fierce wrong ya done that's caught up with ya.

HESTER. What fierce wrong?

CATWOMAN. Don't you by talk me, I'm the Catwoman. I know things. Now I can't say I know the exact wrong ya done but I'd put a bet on it's somethin' serious judgin' by the way ya go on.

HESTER. And what way do I go on?

CATWOMAN. What was it ya done, Hester?

HESTER. I done nothin' — Or if I did I never meant to.

CATWOMAN. There's a fine answer, a half a lie and a half a truth.

HESTER. Everywan has done wrong at wan time or another.

CATWOMAN. Aye but not everywan knows the price of wrong. You do and it's the best thing about ya and there's not much in ya I'd praise. No, most manage to stay a step or two ahead of the pigsty truth of themselves, not you though.

HESTER. Ah, would ya give over. Ya lap up people's fears, you've too much time on your own, concoctin' stories about others. Go way and kill a few mice for your dinner, only lave me alone — Or tell me about me mother, for what I remember doesn't add up.

CATWOMAN. What ya want to know about big Josie Swane?

HESTER. Everythin'.

CATWOMAN. Well, what ya remember?

HESTER. Only small things — Like her pausin'.

CATWOMAN. She was a great wan for the pausin'.

HESTER. "G'wan to bed, you," she'd say, "I'll just be here pausin'." And I'd watch her from the window. *(Indicates window of caravan.)* Times she'd smoke a cigar which she had her own particular way of doin'. She'd hould it stretched away from her and, instead of takin' the cigar to her mouth, she'd bring her mouth to the cigar. And her all the time pausin'. What was she waitin' for, Catwoman? And did she ever find it?

CATWOMAN. Ya'd often hear her voice comin' over the bog at night. She was the greatest song stitcher ever to have passed through this place and we've had plenty pass through but none like Josie Swane. But somewhere along the way she stopped weavin' them songs and became small and bitter and mean. By the time she ran off and left ya I couldn't abide her.

HESTER. There's a longin' in me for her that won't quell this while gone.

CATWOMAN. I wouldn't long for Josie Swane if I was you. Sure the night ya were born she took ya over to the black swan's lair, auld Black Wing ya've just buried there, and laid ya in the nest alongside her. And when I axed her why she'd do a thing like that with snow and ice everywhere, ya know what she says, Swane means swan. That may be so, says I, but the child'll die of pneumonia. That child, says Josie Swane, will live as long as this black swan, not a day more, not a day less. And each night for three nights she left ya in the black swan's lair and each night I snuck ya out of the lair and took ya home with me and brung ya back to the lair before she'd come lookin' for ya in the mornin'. That's when I started to turn again' her.

HESTER. You're makin' it up to get rid of me like everywan else round here. Xavier Cassidy put ya up to this.

CATWOMAN. Xavier Cassidy put me up to nothin'. I'm only tellin' ya so ya know what sourt of a woman your mother was. Ya

14

were lucky she left ya. just forget about her and lave this place now or ya never will.

HESTER. Doesn't seem to make much difference whether I stay or lave with a curse like that on me head.

CATWOMAN. There's ways round curses. Curses only have the power ya allow them. I'm tellin' ya, Hester, ya have to go. When have I ever been proved wrong? Tould ya ya'd have just the wan daughter, tould ya the day and hour she'd be born, didn't I now?

HESTER. Ya did alright.

CATWOMAN. Tould ya Carthage Kilbride was no good for ya, never grew his backbone, would ya listen? Tould Monica Murray to stop her only son drivin' to the city that night. Would she listen? Where's her son? In his grave, that's where he is. Begged her till she ran me off with a kittle of bilin' water. Mayhap she wanted him dead. I'll say nothin'. Gave auld Xavier Cassidy herbs to cure his wife. What did he do? Pegged them down the tilet and took Olive Cassidy to see some swanky medicine man in a private hospital. They cured her alright, cured her so well she came back cured as a side of ham in an oak coffin with golden handles. Maybe he wanted her dead too. There's many gets into brown studies over buryin' their loved wans. That a fact, Hester Swane. I'll be off now and don't say the Catwoman never tould ya. Lave this place now or ya never will.

HESTER. I'm stoppin' here.

CATWOMAN. Sure I know that too. Seen it writ in a bog hole.

HESTER. Is there anythin' them blind eyes doesn't see writ in a bog hole?

CATWOMAN. Sneer away. Ya know what the Catwoman says is true, but sneer away and we'll see will that sneer be on your puss at dusk. Remember the Catwoman then for I don't think I'll have the stomach for this place tonight. (*And exit the Catwoman and exit Hester.*)

Scene 4

Josie and Mrs. Kilbride enter and sit at the garden table as the Catwoman and Hester exit. Josie is dressed: wellingtons, trousers, jumper on inside out. They're playing Snap. Mrs. Kilbride plays ruthlessly, loves to win. Josie looks on in dismay.

MRS. K. Snap — snap! Snap! *(Stacking the cards.)* How many games is that I'm after winnin' ya?

JOSIE. Five.

MRS. K. And how many did you win?

JOSIE. Ya know right well I won ne'er a game.

MRS. K. And do ya know why ya won ne'er a game, Josie? Because you're thick, that's the why.

JOSIE. I always win when I play me Mam.

MRS. K. That's only because your Mam is thicker than you. Thick and stubborn and dangerous wrong-headed and backwards to top it all. Are ya goin' to start cryin' now, ya little pussy babby, don't you dare cry, ya need to toughen up, child, what age are ya now? — I says what age are ya?

JOSIE. Seven.

MRS. K. Seven auld years. When I was seven I was cookin' dinners for a houseful of men, I was thinnin' turnips twelve hour a day, I was birthin' calves, sowin' corn, stookin' hay, ladin' a bull be his nose, and you can't even win a game of Snap. Sit up straight or ya'll grow up a hunchback. Would ya like that, would ya, to grow up a hunchback? Ya'd be like an auld camel and everyone'd say, as ya loped by, there goes Josie Kilbride the hunchback, would ya like that, would ya? Answer me.

JOSIE. Ya know right well I wouldn't, Granny.

MRS. K. What did I tell ya about callin' me Grandmother.

JOSIE. *(Defiantly.)* Granny.

MRS. K. *(Leans over the table viciously.)* Grandmother! Say it!

JOSIE. *(Giving in.)* Grandmother.

MRS. K. And you're lucky I even let ya call me that. Ya want another game?

JOSIE. Only if ya don't cheat.

MRS. K. When did I cheat?

JOSIE. I seen ya, loads of times.

MRS. K. A bad loser's all you are, Josie, and there's nothin' meaner than a bad loser. I never cheat. Never. D'ya hear me, do ya? Look me in the eye when I'm talkin' to ya, ya little bastard. D'ya want another game?

JOSIE. No thanks, Grandmother.

MRS. K. And why don't ya? Because ya know I'll win, isn't that it? Ya little coward ya, I'll break your spirit yet and then glue ya back the way I want ya. I bet ya can't even spell your name.

JOSIE. And I bet ya I can.

MRS. K. G'wan then, spell it.

JOSIE. *(Spells.)* J-o-s-i-e K-i-l-b-r-i-d-e.

MRS. K. Wrong! Wrong! Wrong!

JOSIE. Well, that's the way Teacher taught me.

MRS. K. Are you back-answerin' me?

JOSIE. No, Grandmother.

MRS. K. Ya got some of it right. Ya got the Josie part right, but ya got the Kilbride part wrong, because you're not a Kilbride. You're a Swane. Can ya spell Swane? Of course ya can't. You're Hester Swane's little bastard. You're not a Kilbride and never will be.

JOSIE. I'm tellin' Daddy what ya said.

MRS. K. Tell him! Ya won't be tellin' him anythin' I haven't tould him meself. He's an eegit, your Daddy. I warned him about that wan, Hester Swane, that she'd get her claws in, and she did, the tinker. That's what yees are, tinkers. And your poor Daddy, all he's had to put up with. Well, at least that's all changin' now. Why don't yees head off in that auld caravan, back to wherever yees came from, and give your poor Daddy back to me where he right-fully belongs. And you've your jumper on backwards.

JOSIE. It's not backwards, it's inside out.

MRS. K. Don't you cheek me — and tell me this, Josie Swane, how much has your Mam in the bank?

JOSIE. I don't know.

MRS. K. I'll tell ya how much, a great big goose egg. Useless,

17

that's what she is, livin' off of handouts from my son that she flitters away on whiskey and cigars, the Jezebel witch. *(Smugly.)* Guess how much I've saved, Josie, g'wan, guess, guess.

JOSIE. I wish me Mam'd come soon.

MRS. K. Ah g'wan, child, guess.

JOSIE. Ten pound.

MRS. K. *(Hysterical.)* Ten pound! A'ya mad, child? A'ya mad! Ten pound! *(Whispers avariciously.)* Three thousand pound. All mine. I saved it. I didn't frig it away on crame buns and blouses. No. I saved it. A thousand for me funeral, a thousand for the Little Sisters of the Poor and a thousand for your Daddy. I'm lavin' you nothin' because your mother would get hould of it. And d'ya think would I get any thanks for savin' all that money? Oh no, none, none in the world. Would it ever occur to anywan to say, well done, Mrs. Kilbride, well done, Elsie, not wance did your Daddy ever say, well done, Mother, no, too busy fornicatin' with Hester Swane, too busy bringin' little bastards like yourself into the world.

JOSIE. Can I go and play now?

MRS. K. Here, I brung ya sweets, g'wan ate them, ate them all, there's a great child, ya need some sugar, some sweetie pie sweetness in your life. C'mere and give your auld Grandmother a kiss. *(Josie does.)* Sure it's not your fault ya were born a little girl bastard. D'ya want another game of Snap? I'll let ya win.

JOSIE. No.

MRS. K. Don't you worry, child, we'll get ya off of her yet. Me and your Daddy has plans. We'll batter ya into the semblance of legitimacy yet, soon as we get ya off — *(Enter Carthage.)*

CARTHAGE. I don't know how many times I tould ya to lave the child alone. You've her poisoned with your bile and rage.

MRS. K. I'm sayin' nothin' that isn't true. Can't I play a game of Snap with me own granddaughter?

CARTHAGE. Ya know I don't want ya around here at the minute. G'wan home, Mother, g'wan.

MRS. K. And do what? Talk to the range? Growl at God?

CARTHAGE. Do whatever ya like, only lave Josie alone, pick on somewan your own size. *(Turning Josie's jumper the right way around.)* You'll have to learn to dress yourself.

MRS. K. Ah now, Carthage, don't be annoyed with me. I only

came up to say goodbye to her, found her in her pyjamas out here playin' in the snow. Why isn't her mother mindin' her?

CARTHAGE. Don't start in on that again.

MRS. K. I never left you on your own.

CARTHAGE. Ya should have.

MRS. K. And ya never called in to see the new dress I got for today and ya promised ya would. *(Carthage glares at her.)* Alright, I'm goin', I'm goin'. Just don't think now ya've got Caroline Cassidy ya can do away with me, the same as you're doin' away with Hester Swane. I'm your mother and I won't be goin' away. Ever. *(And exit Mrs. Kilbride.)*

CARTHAGE. Where's your Mam?

JOSIE. Isn't she always on the bog? Can I go to your weddin'?

CARTHAGE. What does your mother say?

JOSIE. She says there'll be no weddin' and to stop annoyin' her.

CARTHAGE. Does she now?

JOSIE. Will you ax her for me?

CARTHAGE. We'll see, Josie, we'll see.

JOSIE. I'll wear me Communion dress. Remember me Communion, Daddy?

CARTHAGE. I do.

JOSIE. Wasn't it just a brilliant day?

CARTHAGE. It was, sweetheart, it was. Come on we go check the calves. *(And exit the pair.)*

Scene 5

Enter Caroline Cassidy in her wedding dress and veil. Twenty, fragile-looking and nervous. She goes to the window of Hester's house and knocks.

CAROLINE. Hester — are ya there? *(Hester comes up behind her.)*

HESTER. Haven't you the gall comin' here, Caroline Cassidy.

CAROLINE. *(Jumps with fright.)* Oh! *(Recovers.)* Can come here

19

whenever I want, this is my house now, sure ya signed it over and all.

HESTER. Bits of paper, writin', means nothin', can as aisy be unsigned.

CAROLINE. You're meant to be gone this week, it's just not fair.

HESTER. Lots of things isn't fair, Daddy's little ice-pop.

CAROLINE. We're goin' ahead with the weddin', me and Carthage, ya think ya'll disrupt everythin', Hester Swane. I'm not afraid of ya.

HESTER. Ya should be. I'm afraid of meself — What is it ya want from me, Caroline? What have I ever done on you that ya feel the need to take everythin' from me?

CAROLINE. I'm takin' nothin' ya haven't lost already and lost this long while gone.

HESTER. You're takin' me husband, you're takin' me house, ya even want me daughter. Over my dead body.

CAROLINE. He was never your husband, he only took pity on ya, took ya out of that auld caravan on the bog, gave ya a home, built ya up from nothin'.

HESTER. Them the sweet nothin's he's been tellin' ya? Let's get wan thing straight, it was me built Carthage Kilbride up from nothin', him a labourer's son you wouldn't give the time of day to and you trottin' by in your first bra, on your half-bred mare, your nose nudgin' the sun. It was me who tould him he could do better. It was my money that bought his first fine acres. It was in my bed he slowly turned from a slavish pup to a man and no frigid little Daddy's girl is goin' to take him from me. Now get off of my property before I cut that dress to ribbons.

CAROLINE. I'll have to get Daddy. He'll run ya off with a shotgun if he has to.

HESTER. Not everyone is as afraid of your Daddy as you are, Caroline.

CAROLINE. Look, I'll give ya more money if ya'll only go. Here's me bank book, there's nearly nineteen thousand pounds in it, me inheritance from me mother. Daddy gave it to me this mornin'. Ya can have it, only please go. It's me weddin' day. It's meant to be happy. It's meant to be the best day of me life. (*She stands there, close to tears. Hester goes over to her, touches her veil.*)

HESTER. What ya want me to do, Caroline? Admire your dress?

20

Wish ya well? Hah? I used babysit you. Remember that?

CAROLINE. That was a long time ago.

HESTER. Not that long at all. After your mother died, several nights ya came down and slept with me. Ya were glad of the auld caravan then, when your Daddy'd be off at the races or the mart or the pub, remember that, do ya? A pasty little thing, and I'd be awake half the night listenin' to your girly gibberish and grievances. Listen to me now, Caroline, there's two Hester Swanes, one that is decent and very fond of ya despite your callow treatment of me. And the other Hester, well, she could slide a knife down your face, carve ya up and not bat an eyelid. *(Grabs her hair suddenly and viciously.)*

CAROLINE. Ow! Lave go!

HESTER. Listen to me now, Caroline. Carthage Kilbride is mine and only mine. He's been mine since he was sixteen. You think ya can take him from me? Wrong. All wrong. *(Lets go of her.)* Now get out of me sight.

CAROLINE. Ya'll be sorry for this, Hester Swane.

HESTER. We all will. *(And exit Caroline, running.)*

Scene 6

Hester lights a cigar, sits at her garden table. Enter Josie with an old shawl around her head and a pair of high heels. She is pretending to be her Granny.

JOSIE. Well good mornin', Tinker Swane.

HESTER. *(Mock surprise.)* Oh, good mornin', Mrs. Kilbride, what a lovely surprise, and how are ya today?

JOSIE. I've been savin' all night.

HESTER. Have ya now, Mrs. Kilbride.

JOSIE. Tell me, ya Jezebel witch, how much have ya in the bank today?

HESTER. Oh, I've three great big goose eggs, Mrs. Kilbride.

21

How much have ya in the bank yourself?

JOSIE. Seventeen million pound. Seventeen million pound. I saved it. I didn't frig it away on love stories and silk stockin's. I cut back on sugar and I cut back on flour. I drank biled socks instead of tay and in wan night I saved seventeen million pound.

HESTER. Ya drank biled socks, Mrs. Kilbride?

JOSIE. I did and I had turf stew for me dinner and for desert I had snail tart and a big mug of wee-wee.

HESTER. Sounds delicious, Mrs. Kilbride.

JOSIE. Ya wouldn't get better in Buckin'am Palace.

HESTER. Josie, don't ever say any of that in front of your Granny, sure ya won't?

JOSIE. I'm not a total eegit, Mam.

HESTER. Did ya have your breakfast?

JOSIE. I had a sugar sammige.

HESTER. Ya better not have.

JOSIE. Granny made me disgustin' porridge.

HESTER. Did she? Did ya wash your teeth?

JOSIE. Why do I always have to wash me teeth? Every day. It's so borin'. What do I need teeth for anyway?

HESTER. Ya need them for snarlin' at people when smilin' doesn't work anymore. G'wan in and wash them now. (*Enter Carthage in his wedding suit, Hester looks at him, looks away.*)

JOSIE. Did ya count the cattle, Daddy?

CARTHAGE. I did.

JOSIE. Were they all there?

CARTHAGE. They were, Josie.

JOSIE. Daddy says I can go to his weddin'.

CARTHAGE. I said maybe, Josie.

HESTER. G'wan round the back and play, Josie.

JOSIE. Can I go, Mam, can I? Say yeah, g'wan, say yeah.

HESTER. We'll see, g'wan, Josie, g'wan, good girl. (*And exit Josie. They both watch her. Silence.*)

CARTHAGE. I'd like to know what ya think you're playin' at.

HESTER. Take a better man than you to cancel me out, Carthage Kilbride.

CARTHAGE. Ya haven't even started packin'.

HESTER. Them your weddin' clothes?

CARTHAGE. They're not me farm clothes, are they?

HESTER. Ya've a cheek comin' here in them.

CARTHAGE. Well, you missus, are meant to be gone.

HESTER. And ya've a nerve tellin' Josie she can go to your weddin'.

CARTHAGE. She's mine as well as yours.

HESTER. Have ya slept with her yet?

CARTHAGE. That's none of your business.

HESTER. Every bit of me business. Ya think ya can wipe out fourteen years just like that. Well she's welcome to ya and any satisfaction she can squeeze out of ya.

CARTHAGE. Never heard ya complainin' when I was in your bed.

HESTER. Ya done the job, I suppose, in a kindergarten sourt of way.

CARTHAGE. Kindergarten, that what ya call it?

HESTER. You were nothin' before I put me stamp on ya and ya'll be nothin' again I'm finished with ya.

CARTHAGE. Are you threatenin' me, Hetty? Because, if ya are, ya better know who you're dealin' with, not the sixteen-year-auld fool snaggin' hares along the Bog of Cats who fell into your clutches.

HESTER. It was you wooed me, Carthage Kilbride, not the other way round as ya'd like everywan to think. In the beginnin' I wanted nothin' to do with ya, should've trusted me first instinct, but ya kept comin' back. You cut your teeth on me, Carthage Kilbride, gnawed and sucked till all that's left is an auld bone ya think to fling on the dunghill, now you've no more use for me. If you think I'm goin' to let you walk over me like that, ya don't know me at all.

CARTHAGE. That at least is true. I've watched ya now for the best part of fourteen years and I can't say for sure I know the first thing about ya. Who are ya and what sourt of stuff are ya made of?

HESTER. The same as you and I can't abide to lose ya. Don't lave me. Don't — is it I've gotten old and you just hittin' thirty?

CARTHAGE. Ya know right well it isn't that.

HESTER. And I haven't had a drink since the night ya left.

CARTHAGE. I know.

HESTER. I only ever drank anyway to forget about —

CARTHAGE. I don't want to talk about that. Lave it.

HESTER. And still ya took the money and bought the land, the Kilbrides who never owned anythin' till I came along, tinker and

23

all. Tell me what to do, Carthage, and I'll do it, anythin' for you to come back.

CARTHAGE. Just stop, will ya —

HESTER. Anythin', Carthage, anythin', and I'll do it if it's in me power.

CARTHAGE. It's not in your power — Look, I'm up to me neck in another life that can't include ya anymore.

HESTER. You're sellin' me and Josie down the river for a few lumpy auld acres and notions of respectability and I never thought ya would. You're better than all of them. Why must ya always look for the good opinion from them that'll never give it? Ya'll only ever be Xavier Cassidy's work horse. He won't treat ya right. He wouldn't know how.

CARTHAGE. He's treatin' me fine, signin' his farm over to me this evenin'.

HESTER. Ya know what they're sayin' about ya? That you're a jumped-up land-hungry mongrel but that Xavier Cassidy is greedier and craftier and he'll spancel ya back to the scrubber ya are.

CARTHAGE. And ya know what they're sayin' about you? That it's time ya moved onto another haltin' site.

HESTER. I was born on the Bog of Cats and on the Bog of Cats I'll end me days. I've as much right to this place as any of yees, more, for it holds me to it in ways it has never held yees. And as for me tinker blood, I'm proud of it. It gives me an edge over all of yees around here, allows me see yees for the inbred, underbred, bog-brained shower yees are. I'm warnin' ya now, Carthage, you go through with this sham weddin' and you'll never see Josie again.

CARTHAGE. If I have to mow ya down or have ya declared an unfit mother to see Josie I will, so for your own sake don't cause any trouble in that department. Look, Hetty, I want Josie to do well in the world, she'll get her share of everythin' I own and will own. I want her to have a chance in life, a chance you never had and so can never understand —

HESTER. Don't tell me what I can and can't understand!

CARTHAGE. Well understand this. Ya'll not separate me and Josie or I'll have her taken off of ya. I only have to mention your drinkin' or your night roamin' or the way ya sleep in that dirty auld caravan and lave Josie alone in the house.

HESTER. I always take Josie to the caravan when I sleep there.

CARTHAGE. Ya didn't take her last night.

HESTER. I wasn't in the caravan last night. I was walkin' the bog, but I checked on her three, four times.

CARTHAGE. Just don't cross me with Josie because I don't want to have to take her off of ya, I know she's attached to ya, and I'm not a monster. Just don't cross me over her or I'll come down on ya like a bull from heaven.

HESTER. So I'm meant to lie back and let Caroline Cassidy have her way in the rearin' of me child. I'm meant to lave her around Xavier Cassidy — sure he's capable of anythin'. If it's the last thing I do I'll find a way to keep her from ya.

CARTHAGE. I want you out of here before dusk! And I've put it to ya now about Josie. Think it over when ya've calmed down. And here. *(Producing envelope.)* There's your blood money. It's all there down to the last penny.

HESTER. No! I don't want it!

CARTHAGE. *(Throws it in the snow.)* Neither do I. I never should've took it in the first place. I owe ya nothin' now, Hester Swane. Nothin'. Ya've no hold over me now. *(Goes to exit.)*

HESTER. Carthage — ya can't just walk away like this.

CARTHAGE. I can and I am — Ya know what amazes me, Hetty?

HESTER. What?

CARTHAGE. That I stayed with ya so long — I want peace, just peace — Remember, before dusk. *(And exit Carthage. Hester looks after him, a low heartbroken wail. Josie comes running on.)*

JOSIE. What's wrong of ya, Mam?

HESTER. Ah go 'way, would ya, and lave me alone.

JOSIE. Can I go down to Daly's and buy sweets?

HESTER. No, ya can't. Go on off and play, you're far too demandin'.

JOSIE. Yeah well, just because you're in a bad humour it's not my fault. I'm fed up playin' on me own.

HESTER. You'll get a clatter if you're not careful. I played on me own when I was your age, I never bothered me mother, you're spoilt rotten, that's what ya are. *(In a gentler tone.)* G'wan and play with your dolls, give them a bath, cut their hair.

JOSIE. Ya said I wasn't to cut their hair.

HESTER. Well now I'm sayin' ya can, alright.

JOSIE. But it won't grow back.

HESTER. So! There's worse things in this world than your dolls' hair not growin' back, believe me, Josie Swane.

JOSIE. Me name is Josie Kilbride.

HESTER. That's what I said.

JOSIE. Ya didn't, ya said Josie Swane. I'm not a Swane. I'm a Kilbride.

HESTER. I suppose you're ashamed of me too. *(Enter Xavier Cassidy and Caroline, both in their wedding clothes.)*

JOSIE. Caroline, your dress, is that your weddin' dress? It's beautiful.

CAROLINE. Hello Josie. *(Josie runs over to Caroline to touch her dress. Hester storms after her, picks her up roughly, carries her to corner of the house. Puts her down.)*

HESTER. Now stay around the back. *(And exit Josie.)*

XAVIER. Was hopin' I wouldn't find ya still here, Swane.

HESTER. So ya came back with your Daddy, ya know nothin', Caroline, nothin'. *(Sits at her garden table, produces a naggin of whiskey from her pocket, drinks.)*

XAVIER. Thought ya'd given up the drink.

HESTER. I had. Me first in months, but why should I try and explain meself to you?

XAVIER. Might interest Carthage to know you lashin' into a naggin of whiskey at this hour.

HESTER. Carthage. If it wasn't for you, me and Carthage'd be fine. Should've eradicated ya, Cassidy, when I could've. God's punishin' me now because I didn't take steps that were right and proper concernin' you. Aye. God's punishin' me but I won't take his blows lyin' down.

CAROLINE. What are ya talking about, Hester?

HESTER. What am I talkin' about? I'm talkin' about you, ya little fool, and I'm talkin' about James.

CAROLINE. Me brother James?

XAVIER. You keep a civil tongue, Swane, over things ya know nothin' about.

HESTER. Oh, but I do know things, and that's why ya want me

out of here. It's only your land and money and people's fear of ya that has ya walkin' free. G'wan home and do whatever it is ya do with your daughter, but keep your sleazy eyes off of me and Josie. This is my property and I've a right to sit in me own yard without bein' ogled by the likes of you.

XAVIER. There's things softer on the eye than you, Swane, if it's oglin' I was after. This is no longer your property and well ya know it, ya signed it over six months ago, for a fine hefty sum, have the papers here.

HESTER. I wasn't thinkin' right then, was bein' coerced and bullied from all sides, but I have regained me pride and it tells me I'm stayin'. Ya'll get your money back. *(Picks up envelope Carthage has thrown in the snow.)* Here's some of it.

XAVIER. I'm not takin' it. A deal's a deal.

HESTER. Take it! Take it! *(Stuffs it into his breast pocket.)* And it might interest ya to know, Caroline, that Carthage was just here in his weddin' clothes and he didn't look like no radiant groom and he axed me to take him back, but I said —

XAVIER. I'd say he did alright —

HESTER. He did! He did! Or as much as, but I said I couldn't be played with anymore, that I was made for things he has lost the power to offer. And I was. I was made for somethin' different than these butchery lives yees all lead here on the Bog of Cats. Me mother taught me that.

XAVIER. Your mother. Your mother taught ya nothin', Swane, except maybe how to use a knife. Let me tell ya a thing or two about your mother, big Josie Swane. I used see her outside her auld caravan on the bog and the fields covered over in stars and her half covered in an excuse for a dress and her croonin' towards Orion in a language I never heard before or since. We'd peace when she left.

HESTER. And what were ya doin' watchin' her? Catwoman tould me ya were in a constant swoon over me mother, sniffin' round the caravan, lavin' little presents and Christmas dinners and money and drink, sure I remember the gatch of ya meself and ya scrapin' at the door.

XAVIER. Very presumptuous of ya, Swane, to think I'd have any interest in your mother beyond Christian compassion.

HESTER. Christian compassion! That what it's called these days!

XAVIER. Aye, Christian compassion, a thing that was never bet into you. Ya say ya remember lots of things, then maybe ya remember that that food and money I used lave was left so ya wouldn't starve. Times I'd walk by that caravan and there'd be ne'er a sign of this mother of yours. She'd go off for days with anywan who'd buy her a drink. She'd be off in the bars of Pullagh and Mucklagh gettin' into fights. Wance she bit the nose off a woman who dared to look at her man, bit the nose clean off her face. And you, you'd be chained to the door of the caravan with maybe a dirty nappy on ya if ya were lucky. Often times —
HESTER. Lies! All lies!
XAVIER. Often times I brung ya home and gave ya over to me mother to put some clothes on ya and feed ya. More times than I can remember it'd be from our house your mother would collect ya, the brazen walk of her, and not a thank you or a flicker of guilt in her eye and her reekin' of drink. Times she wouldn't even bother to collect ya and meself or me mother would have to bring ya down to her and she'd hardly notice that we'd come and gone or that you'd returned.
HESTER. Ya expect me to believe anythin' that comes from your siled lips, Xavier Cassidy.
XAVIER. And wan other thing, Swane, for you to cast aspersions on me just because I'm an auld widower, that's cheap and low. Not everywan sees the world through your troubled eyes. There's such a thing as a father lovin' his daughter as a father should, no more, no less, somethin' you have never known, and I will —
HESTER. I had a father too! Ya'd swear I was dropped from the sky the way ya go on. Jack Swane of Bergit's Island, I never knew him — but I had a father. I'm as settled as any of yees —
XAVIER. Well, he wasn't much of a father, never claimin' ya when your mother ran off.
HESTER. He claimed me in the end —
XAVIER. Look, Swane, I don't care about your family or where ya came from. I care only about me own and all I've left is Caroline and if I have to plough through you to have the best for her, then that's what I'll do. I don't want to unless I have to. So do it the aisy way for all of us. Lave this place today. (Takes envelope from breast pocket, puts it into her hand.) This is yours. Come on, Caroline.

CAROLINE. Ya heard what Daddy says. Ya don't know his temper, Hester.

HESTER. And you don't know mine. *(And exit Xavier followed by Caroline. Hester sits at her garden table, has a drink, looks up at the cold winter sky. A whisper.)* Dear God on high, what have ya in store for me at all? *(Enter Josie in her Communion dress, veil, buckled shoes, handbag, the works. Looks at her a minute.)* What are ya doin' in your Communion dress?

JOSIE. For Daddy's weddin'. I'm grown out of all me other dresses.

HESTER. I don't think ya are.

JOSIE. I am. I can go, can't I, Mam?

HESTER. Ya have her eyes.

JOSIE. Whose eyes — whose eyes, Mam?

HESTER. Josie Swane's, me mother.

JOSIE. Granny said me real name is Josie Swane.

HESTER. Don't mind your Granny.

JOSIE. Did ya like her, Josie Swane?

HESTER. — More than anythin' in this cold white world.

JOSIE. More than me and Daddy?

HESTER. I'm talkin' about when I was your age. Ya weren't born then, Josie — Ya know the last time I saw me mother I was wearin' me Communion dress too, down by the caravan, a beautiful summer's night and the bog like a furnace. I wouldn't go to bed though she kept tellin' me to. I don't know why I wouldn't, I always done what she tould me. I think now — maybe I knew. And she says, I'm goin' walkin' the bog, you're to stay here, Hetty. And I says, No, I'd go along with her, and made to folly her. And she says, No, Hetty, you wait here, I'll be back in a while. And again I made to folly her and again she stopped me. And I watched her walk away from me across the Bog of Cats. And across the Bog of Cats I'll watch her return. *(Lights down.)*

29

ACT TWO

Interior of Xavier Cassidy's house. A long table covered in a white tablecloth, laid for the wedding feast. Music off, a band setting up. The Catwoman sits at centre table lapping wine from a saucer. A waiter, a lanky, gawky young fellow, hovers with a bottle of wine waiting to refill the saucer.

WAITER. You're sure now ya wouldn't like a glass, Catwoman?

CATWOMAN. No, no, I love the saucer, young man. What's your name? Do I know ya?

WAITER. I'm a Dunne.

CATWOMAN. Wan of the long Dunnes or wan of the scutty fat-legged Dunnes?

WAITER. Wan of the long Dunnes. Ya want a refill, Catwoman?

CATWOMAN. I will. Are ya still in school? Your voice sounds as if it's just breakin'.

WAITER. I am.

CATWOMAN. And what're ya goin' to be when ya grow up, young Long Dunne?

WAITER. I want to be an astronaut but me father wants me to work on the bog like him and like me grandfather. The Dunnes has always worked on the bog.

CATWOMAN. Oh go for the astronaut, young man.

WAITER. I will so, Catwoman. Have ya enough wine?

CATWOMAN. Plenty for now. (*Exit young Dunne crossed by the ghost of Joseph Swane, entering; blood-stained shirt and trousers, a throat wound. He walks across the stage. Catwoman cocks her ear, starts sniffing.*)

JOSEPH. Hello. Hello.

CATWOMAN. Ah Christ, not another ghost.

JOSEPH. Who's there?

CATWOMAN. Go 'way and lave me alone. I'm on me day off.

JOSEPH. Who are ya? I can't see ya.

CATWOMAN. I can't see you aither. I'm the Catwoman but I tould ya I'm not talkin' to ghosts today, yees have me heart scalded, hardly got a wink's sleep last night.

JOSEPH. Please, I haven't spoken to anywan since the night I died.

CATWOMAN. Haven't ya? Who are ya anyway?

JOSEPH. I'm Joseph Swane of Bergit's Island. Is this Bergit's Island?

CATWOMAN. This is the Bog of Cats.

JOSEPH. The Bog of Cats. Me mother had a song about this place.

CATWOMAN. Josie Swane was your mother?

JOSEPH. Ya know her?

CATWOMAN. Oh aye, I knew her. Then Hester must be your sister?

JOSEPH. Hester, ya know Hester too?

CATWOMAN. She lives only down the lane. I never knew Hester had a brother.

JOSEPH. I doubt she'd be tellin' people about me.

CATWOMAN. I don't mean to be short with ya, Joseph Swane, but Saturday is me day off. I haven't a minute to meself with yees, so tell me what is it ya want and then be on your way.

JOSEPH. I want to be alive again. I want to stop walkin'. I want to rest, ate a steak, meet a girl, I want to fish for wild salmon and sow pike on Bergit's Lake again.

CATWOMAN. You'll never do them things again, Joseph Swane.

JOSEPH. Don't say that to me, Catwoman, I'm just turned eighteen.

CATWOMAN. Eighteen. That's young to die alright. But it could be worse. I've a two-year-old ghost who comes to visit, all she wants to do is play Peep. Still eighteen's young enough. How come ya went so young? An accident, was it? Or by your own hand?

WAITER. (Going by.) Ya talkin' to me, Catwoman?

CATWOMAN. No, Long Dunne, just a ghost, a poor lost ghost.

WAITER. Oh. (And exit.)

JOSEPH. Are ya still there, Catwoman?

31

CATWOMAN. I am but there's nothin' I can do for ya, you're not comin' back.

JOSEPH. Is there no way?

CATWOMAN. None, none in this world anyway, and the sooner ya realize that the better for ya. Now be on your way, settle in to your new world, knock the best out of it ya can.

JOSEPH. It's fierce hard to knock the best out of nothin', fierce hard to enjoy darkness the whole time, can't I just stay here with ya, talk to ya a while?

CATWOMAN. Ya could I suppose, only I'm at a weddin' and they might think I'm not the full shillin' if I have to be talkin' to you all day. Look, I'll take ya down to Hester Swane's house, ya can talk to her.

JOSEPH. Can she hear ghosts?

CATWOMAN. (Getting up.) Oh aye, though she lets on she can't.

JOSEPH. Alright so, I suppose I may as well since I'm here.

CATWOMAN. C'mon, folly me voice till I lead ya there.

JOSEPH. (Following her.) Keep talkin' so I don't take a wrong turnin'.

CATWOMAN. I will and hurry up now, I don't want to miss the weddin'. Ya still there?

JOSEPH. I am. (And they're off by now. Enter Caroline and Carthage as they exit.)

CAROLINE. This is the tablecloth me mother had for her weddin' and it's the same silver too. I'd really like for her to have been here today — Aye, I would.

CARTHAGE. A soft-boned lady, your mother. I used see her in town shoppin' with you be the hand, ya wanted to bow when she walked by, she had class. And you have too, Caroline, like no wan else around here.

CAROLINE. I can't stop thinkin' about Hester.

CARTHAGE. (Kisses her.) Hester'll be fine, tough as an auld boot. Ya shouldn't concern yourself with her on your weddin' day. I've provided well for her, she isn't goin' to ever have to work a day in her life. Josie's the wan I worry about. The little sweetheart all done up in her Communion dress. Hetty should've got her a proper dress.

CAROLINE. But Hester didn't want her here, Carthage.

CARTHAGE. Ya know what I wish?

CAROLINE. What?

CARTHAGE. That she'd just give Josie to me and be done with it.

CAROLINE. You're still very tangled up with Hester, aren't ya?

CARTHAGE. I'm not wan bit tangled with her, if she'd just do what she's supposed to do which is fierce simple, clear out of the Bog of Cats for wance and for all.

CAROLINE. And I suppose ya'll talk about me as callously wan day too.

CARTHAGE. Of course I won't, why would I?

CAROLINE. It's all fierce messy, Carthage. I'd hoped ya'd have sourted it out by today. It laves me in a fierce awkward position. You're far more attached to her than ya'd led me to believe.

CARTHAGE. Attached to her? I'm not attached to her, I stopped lovin' her years ago!

CAROLINE. I'm not jealous as to whether ya love her or don't love her, I think maybe I'd prefer if ya still did.

CARTHAGE. Then what's botherin' ya?

CAROLINE. You and Hester has a whole history together, stretchin' back years that connects yees and that seems more important and real than anythin' we have. And I wonder have we done the wrong thing.

CARTHAGE. Ya should've said all this before ya took your vows at the altar.

CAROLINE. I've been tryin' to say it to ya for weeks.

CARTHAGE. So what do we do now?

CAROLINE. Get through today, I suppose, pretend it's the best day of our lives. I don't know about you but I've had better days than today, far better.

CARTHAGE. Caroline, what's wrong of ya?

CAROLINE. Nothin' only I feel like I'm walkin' on somewan's grave. (*Enter Mrs. Kilbride in what looks extremely like a wedding dress, white, a white hat, with a bit of a veil trailing off it, white shoes, tights, bag, etc.*)

MRS. K. (*Flushed, excited, neurotic.*) Oh the love birds! The love birds! There yees are, off hidin'. Carthage, I want a photo of yees. Would you take it, Caroline?

33

CARTHAGE. She means she wants wan of herself.

MRS. K. Shush now, Carthage, and stand up straight. *(They pose like a bride and groom, Carthage glaring at Mrs. Kilbride.)* That's it. Wan more, smile, Carthage, smile, I hate a glowery demeanour in a photograph. That's great, Caroline, did ya get me shoes in?

CAROLINE. I don't think I —

MRS. K. Doesn't matter, doesn't matter, thank ya, what a glorious day, what a glorious white winter's day, nothin' must spoil today for me, nothin'. *(Begins photographing her shoes, first one, then the other.)*

CARTHAGE. What in the name of God are ya at now?

MRS. K. I just want to get a photo of me shoes while they're new and clean. I've never had such a beautiful pair of shoes, look at the diamonds sparklin' on them. I saved like a Shylock for them, seen them in O'Brien's six months ago and I knew instantly them were to be me weddin' shoes. And I put by every week for them. Guess how much they were, Carthage, g'wan guess, Caroline, guess, guess.

CAROLINE. I don't know, Mrs. Kilbride.

MRS. K. Elsie! Elsie! Call me Elsie, ah g'wan guess.

CAROLINE. Fifty pound.

MRS. K. *(Angrily.)* Fifty pound! Are ya mad! Are ya out of your tiny mind!

CARTHAGE. Tell us how much they were, Mother, before we die of the suspense.

MRS. K. *(Smug, can hardly believe it herself.)* A hundred and fifty pound. The Quane herself wouldn't pay more. *(Monica and Xavier have entered, Monica has Josie by the hand.)*

MONICA. — And Father Willow seems to have lost the run of himself entirely.

XAVIER. They should put him down, he's eighty if he's a day.

MONICA. The state of him with his hat on all durin' the Mass and the vestments inside out and his pyjamas peepin' out from under his trousers.

XAVIER. Did you hear he's started keepin' a gun in the tabernacle?

MONICA. I did, aye.

XAVIER. For all them robbers, is it?

MONICA. No, apparently it's for any of us that's late for Mass. Ya know what I was thinkin' and I lookin' at Caroline up there on the altar, I was thinkin' about my young fella Brian and I decided not to think about him today at all.

XAVIER. God rest him.

MONICA. If only I'd heeded the Catwoman he'd be here today. Didn't you think about your own young fella too?

XAVIER. Never, I never think about him. Never. Children! If they were calves we'd have them fattened and sould in three weeks. I never think of James. Never.

MONICA. Or Olive aither?

XAVIER. Ah, Olive had no fight in her, wailed like a ewe in a storm after the young lad and then lay down with her face to the wall. Ya know what she died of, Monica? Spite. Spite again' me. Well, she's the wan who's dead. I've the last laugh on her.

MONICA. Strange what these weddin's drag up.

XAVIER. Aye, they cost a fortune. *(Takes two glasses of champagne from a passing waiter.)* Here, Monica, and cheers. *(To Josie.)* Child, a pound for your handbag.

MRS. K. What d'ya say, Josie?

XAVIER. Lave her. Two things in this world get ya nowhere, sayin' sorry and sayin' thanks — that right, Josie?

JOSIE. That's right, Mr. Cassidy.

MRS. K. *(Taking Josie a little aside.)* Here give me that pound till I mind it for ya.

JOSIE. First give me back me Communion money.

MRS. K. What Communion money?

CARTHAGE. So it was you took her Communion money. *(The Catwoman and Father Willow have entered, linking arms, both with their sticks. Father Willow has his snuff on hand, pyjamas showing from under his shirt and trousers, hat on, adores the Catwoman.)*

FATHER WILLOW. I'm tellin' ya now, Catwoman, ya'll have to cut back on the mice, they'll be the death of ya.

CATWOMAN. And you'll have to cut back on the snuff.

FATHER WILLOW. Try snails instead, far better for ya, the French ate them with garlic and tons of butter and Burgundy wine. I tried them wance meself and I in Avalon. Delicious.

CATWOMAN. We should go on a holiday, you and me, Father Willow.

FATHER WILLOW. Ah, ya say that every winter and come the

summer I can't budge ya.

CATWOMAN. I'll go away with ya next summer and that's a promise.

FATHER WILLOW. Well, where do ya want to go and I'll book the tickets in the mornin'?

CATWOMAN. Anywhere at all away from this auld bog, somewhere with a big hot sun.

FATHER WILLOW. Burgundy's your man then.

MONICA. God help Burgundy is all I say.

CATWOMAN. Anywhere it's not rainin' because it's goin' to rain here all next summer, seen it writ in the sky.

MRS. K. Writ in the sky, me eye, sure she's blind as a bat. Xavier, what did ya have to invite the Catwoman for? Brings down the tone of the whole weddin'.

MONICA. Hasn't she as much right to walk God's earth as you, partake of its pleasures too.

MRS. K. No, she hasn't! Not till she washes herself. The turf-smoke stink of her. Look at her moochin' up to Father Willow and her never inside the door of the church and me at seven Mass every mornin' watchin' that auld fool dribblin' into the chalice. And would he call to see me? Never. Spends all his time with the Catwoman in her dirty little hovel. I'd write to the Archbishop if I thought he was capable of anythin'. Why did ya have to invite her?

XAVIER. Ya know as well as me it's bad luck not to invite the Catwoman. *(Father Willow shoots Mrs. Kilbride in the back of the head with an imaginary pistol as he walks by or as she walks by.)*

MRS. K. I'd love to hose her down, fling her in onto the milkin' parlour floor, turn the water on full blast and hose her down to her kidneys.

CARTHAGE. *(With his arm around Caroline.)* Well, Catwoman, what do ya predict for us?

CATWOMAN. I predict nothin'.

CARTHAGE. Ah g'wan now, ya must have a blessin' or a vision or somethin'.

CAROLINE. Lave it, Carthage. You're welcome, Catwoman and Father Willow.

FATHER WILLOW. Thank you, Hester, thank you.

CARTHAGE. You mean, Caroline, Father Willow, this is Caroline.

FATHER WILLOW. Whatever.

CARTHAGE. Come on now, Catwoman, and give Caroline and me wan of your blessin's.

CATWOMAN. Seein' as ya insist. Separate tombstones. I'm sorry but I tould ya not to ax me.

JOSIE. Granny, will ya take a photo of just me and Daddy for to put in me scrapbook?

MRS. K. Don't be so rude, you, to Caroline. *(Hisses.)* And I tould ya to call me Grandmother!

JOSIE. *(Whispers boldly from the safety of her father's side.)* Granny, Granny, Granny.

CAROLINE. She's alright. Here, I'll take the photo of you and Carthage for your scrapbook. *(Does.)*

MRS. K. She's ruined, that's what she is, turnin' up in her Communion dress, makin' a holy show of us all.

CARTHAGE. It's you that's the holy show in that stupid dress.

MRS. K. What! I am not! There's gratitude for ya. Ya make an effort to look your best. *(Close to tears.)* I cut back on everythin' to buy this dress. How was I supposed to know the bride'd be wearin' white as well.

CARTHAGE. Don't start whingin' now in front of everywan, sit down will ya, ya look fine, ya look great — Alright, I'm sorry. Ya look stunnin'!

MRS. K. *(Beginning to smile.)* I don't, do I?

CARTHAGE. Christ! *Yes!*

FATHER WILLOW. *(Leading the Catwoman to the table, whispers to her.)* If ya were a bar of chocolate I'd ate ya.

CATWOMAN. If I was a bar of chocolate I'd ate meself. *(They've all made their way to the table by now and are seated, Xavier tinkles his glass for silence.)*

XAVIER. Thank you. Now before we dig in I'd like to welcome yees all here on wan of the happiest days of me life. Yees have all long known that Caroline has been my greatest joy and reason for livin'. Her mother, if she was here today, would've been proud too at how she has grown into a lovely and graceful woman. I can take no credit for that, though I've taken the greatest pride these long years in watchin' her change from a motherless child to a gawky girl, to this apparition I see before me eyes today. We auld fathers

37

would like to keep our daughters be our sides forever and enjoy their care and gentleness but it seems the world does have a different plan entirely. We must rear them up for another man's benefit. Well if this is so, I can't think of a better man than Carthage Kilbride to take over the care of me only child. *(Raises his glass.)* I wish yees well and happiness and infants rompin' on the hearth.

ALL. Hear! Hear!

XAVIER. Father Willow, would ya do us the —

MRS. K. *(Standing up.)* I'd like to say a few words too —

XAVIER. Go ahead, Mrs. Kilbride.

MRS. K. As the proud mother of the groom —

CARTHAGE. Mother, would ya whisht up —

MRS. K. *(Posh public speaking voice.)* As the proud mother of the groom, I feel the need to answer Xavier's fine speech with a few words of me own. Never was a mother more blessed than me in havin' Carthage for a son. As a child he was uncommon good, never cried, never disobeyed, never raised his voice wance to me, never went about with a grumpy puss on him. Indeed he went to the greatest pains always to see that me spirits was good, that me heart was uplifted. When his father died he used come into the bed to sleep beside me for fear I would be lonely. Often I woke from a deep slumber and his two arms would be around me, a small leg thrown over me in sleep —

CATWOMAN. The craythur —

MRS. K. He was also always aware of my abidin' love for Our Lord, unlike some here *(Glares at the Catwoman.)* and on wan occasion, me birthday it was, I looked out the back window and there he was up on the slope behind our house and what was he doin'? He was buildin' Calvary for me. He'd hammered three wooden crosses and was erectin' them on the slope Calvary-style. Wan for him, wan for me and wan for Our Lord. And we draped ourselves around them like the two thieves in the holy book, remember, Carthage?

CARTHAGE. I do not, would ya ever sit down.

MRS. K. Of course ya do, the three crosses ya made up on the slope and remember the wind was howlin' and the pair of us yellin' "Calvary! Calvary!" to wan another. Of course ya remember. I'm only tellin' yees this story as wan of the countless examples of

38

Carthage's kind nature and I only want to say that Caroline is very welcome into the Kilbride household. And that if Carthage will be as good a son to Caroline as he's been a husband to me then she'll have no complaints. *(Raises her glass.)* Cheers.

ALL. Hear! Hear!

XAVIER. And now, Father Willow, ya'll say grace for us?

FATHER WILLOW. It'd be an honour, Jack, thank you —

MRS. K. Who's Jack?

FATHER WILLOW. *(Getting up.)* In the name of the Father and of the Son and of the Holy Ghost, it may or may not surprise yees all if I tould yees I was almost a groom meself wance. Her name was Elizabeth Kennedy, no that was me mother's name, her name was — it'll come to me, anyway it wasn't to be, in the end we fell out over a duck egg on a walkin' holiday by the Shannon, what was her name at all? Helen? No.

MRS. K. Would ya say the grace, Father Willow, and be —

FATHER WILLOW. The grace, yes, how does it go again?

MRS. K. Bless us, oh Lord, and these thy gifts which of —

FATHER WILLOW. Rowena. That was it. Rowena Phelan. I should never have ate that duck egg — no — *(Stands there lost in thought. Enter Hester in her wedding dress, veil, shoes, the works.)*

MRS. K. Ya piebald knacker ya.

XAVIER. What's your business here, Swane, besides puttin' a curse on me daughter's weddin'?

MRS. K. The brazen nerve of her turnin' up in that garb.

HESTER. The kettle callin' the pot white. Remember this dress, Carthage? He bought it for me —

CAROLINE. Daddy, would ya do somethin'.

HESTER. Oh must be near nine year ago. We'd got to the stage where we should've parted and I said it to ya and ya convinced me otherwise and axed me to marry ya. Came home wan evenin' with this dress in a box and somehow it got put away. Ya only ever wanted me there until ya were strong enough to lave me.

CARTHAGE. Get outa here right now!

HESTER. Ya thought ya could come swaggerin' to me this mornin' in your weddin' clothes, well, here I am in mine. This is my weddin' day be rights and not wan of yees can deny it. And yees all just sit there glarin' as if I'm the guilty wan. *(Takes*

Carthage's glass of wine, drinks from it.)
MRS. K. Run her off, Xavier! Run her off or I will. *(Gets up.)*
CARTHAGE. *(Pulls her back.)* Would you keep out of this!
MRS. K. And let her walk all over us?
MONICA. Hester, go home, g'wan.
MRS. K. *(Getting up again.)* I've had the measure of you this long time, the lazy shiftless blood in ya, that savage tinker eye ya turn on people to frighten them —
CARTHAGE. Would ya shut up! Ya haven't shut up all day! We're not havin' a brawl here.
MRS. K. There's a nice way to talk to your mother on your weddin' day, I'm not afraid of ya, Hester Swane, you're just a sad lost little woman —
HESTER. I still stole your son from ya, didn't I, Elsie? Your sissy boy that I tried to make a man of.
MRS. K. Ya took advantage of him, ya had to take advantage of a young boy for your perverted pleasures for no grown man would stomach ya.
HESTER. And weren't they great, Carthage, all them nights in the caravan I "took advantage" of ya and you bangin' on the window and us stuffin' pillows in our mouths so ya wouldn't hear us laughin' —
MRS. K. You're absolutely disgustin', that's what ya are!
HESTER. Have you ever been discarded, Elsie Kilbride? — the way I've been dis —
MRS. K. No, I've never been discarded, Hester Swane! Ya know why? Because I've never overstepped meself. I've always lived be the rules.
HESTER. Ah rules! What rules are they? Teach them to me and I'll live by them. Yees don't know what it's like, to be flung on the ashpit and you still alive —
XAVIER. No wan's flingin' ya anywhere! We done everythin' proper by you —
HESTER. Proper! Yees have taken everythin' from me. I've done nothin' again' any of yees. I'm just bein' who I am, Carthage, I'm axin' ya the wance more, come away with me now, with me and —
MRS. K. Come away with her, she says —
HESTER. Yes! Come away with me and Josie and stop all this —

40

XAVIER. Come away with ya! Are ya mad! He's married to Caroline now —

CARTHAGE. Go home, Hester, and pack your things.

MONICA. C'mon, Hester, I'll take ya home.

HESTER. I have no home anymore for he's decided to take it from me.

MONICA. Then come and live with me, I've no wan —

HESTER. No, I want to stay in me own house. Just let me stay in the house, Carthage. I won't bother any wan if yees'd just lave me alone. I was born on the Bog of Cats, same as all of yees, though ya'd never think it the way yees shun me. I know every barrow and rivulet and bog hole of its nine square mile. I know where the best bog rosemary grows and the sweetest wild bog rue. I could lead yees around the Bog of Cats in me sleep.

CARTHAGE. There's a house bought and furnished for ya in town as ya agreed to —

HESTER. I've never lived in a town. I won't know anywan there —

MONICA. Ah, let her stay in the house, the Bog of Cats is all she knows —

MRS. K. And since when do we need you stickin' your snout in, Monica Murray?

MONICA. Since you and your son have forgotten all dacency, Elsie Kilbride. Ya've always been too hard on her. Ya never gave her a chance —

MRS. K. A waste of time givin' chances to a tinker. All tinkers understands is the open road and where the next bottle of whiskey is comin' from.

MONICA. Well, you should know and your own grandfather wan!

MRS. K. My grandfather was a wanderin' tinsmith —

MONICA. And what's that but a tinker with notions!

FATHER WILLOW. What year is this wine?

MONICA. Go home, Hester. Don't plead your case with this shower. They'd sicken ya!

HESTER. Carthage, ya could aisy afford another house for yourself and Caroline if ya wanted —

CARTHAGE. No! We're stickin' by what we agreed on —

HESTER. The truth is you want to eradicate me, make out I

41

never existed —

CARTHAGE. If I wanted to eradicate ya, I could've, long ago. And I could've taken Josie off of ya. Facts are, I been more than generous with ya.

HESTER. You're plentiful with the guilt money alright, showerin' buckets of it on me. *(Flings envelope he had given her in Act One at him.)* There's your auld blood money back. Ya think you're gettin' away that aisy! Money won't take that guilt away, Carthage, we'll go to our grave with it!

CARTHAGE. I've not an ounce of guilt where you're concerned and whatever leftover feelin' I had for ya as the mother of me child is gone after this display of hatred towards me. Just go away, I can't bear the sight of ya!

HESTER. I can't lave the Bog of Cats —

MRS. K. We'll burn ya out if we have to —

HESTER. Ya see —

MRS. K. Won't we, Xavier —

XAVIER. Ya can lave me out of any low-boy tactics. You're lavin' this place today, Swane, aren't ya?

HESTER. I can't lave — Ya see me mother said she'd come back here —

MRS. K. Your mother! That tramp hasn't been seen round here in over thirty —

HESTER. Don't call her that! Father Willow, tell them what they're doin' is wrong. They'll listen to you.

FATHER WILLOW. They've never listened to me, sure they even lie in the confession box. Ya know what I do? I wear earplugs.

HESTER. *(Close to tears.)* I can't lave till me mother comes. I'd hoped she'd have come before now and it wouldn't come to this. Don't make me lave this place or somethin' terrible'll happen. Don't.

XAVIER. We've had enough of your ravin', Swane, so take yourself elsewhere and let us try to recoup these marred celebrations.

JOSIE. I'll go with ya, Mam, and ya look gorgeous in that dress.

CARTHAGE. Stay where ya are, Josie.

JOSIE. No, I want to go with me Mam.

CARTHAGE. *(Stopping her.)* Ya don't know what ya want. And reconsiderin', I think it'd be better all round if Josie stays with me till ya've moved. I'll bring her back to ya then.

HESTER. I've swallyed all me pride over you. You're lavin' me no choice but a vicious war against ya. *(Takes a bottle of wine from the table.)* Josie, I'll be back to collect ya later. And you just try keepin' her from me! *(And exit Hester.)*

ACT THREE

Dusk. Hester, in her wedding dress, charred and muddied. Behind her, the house and sheds ablaze. Joseph Swane stands in the flames watching her.

HESTER. Well, Carthage, ya think them were only idle threats I made? Ya think I can be flung in a bog hole like a bag of newborn pups? Let's see how ya like this — Ya hear that sound? Them's your cattle howlin'. Ya smell that smell? That's your forty calves roastin'. I tied them all in and flung diesel on them. And the house, I burnt the bed and the whole place went up in flames. I'd burn down the world if I'd enough diesel — Will somewan not come and save me from meself before I go and do worse. *(Joseph starts to sing.)*
JOSEPH.
By the Bog of Cats I finally learned false from true,
Learned too late that it was you and only you
Left me sore, a heart brimful of rue
By the Bog of Cats in the —
HESTER. Who's there? Who dares sing that song? That's my song that me mother made up for me. Who's there?
JOSEPH. I think ya know me, Hester.
HESTER. It's not Joseph Swane, is it?
JOSEPH. It is alright.
HESTER. I thought I done away with you. Where are ya? I can't see ya. Keep off! Keep away! I'm warnin' ya.
JOSEPH. I'm not here to harm ya.
HESTER. Ya should be. If you'd done to me what I done to you I'd want your guts on a platter. Well come on! I'm ready for ya! Where are ya!
JOSEPH. I don't know, somewhere near ya. I can't see you aither.
HESTER. Well, what do ya want, Joseph Swane, if you're not here to harm me? Is it an apology you're after? Well, I've none for

44

ya. I'd slit your throat again if ya stood here in front of me in flesh and bone.

JOSEPH. Would ya? What're ya so angry about? I've been listenin' to ya screamin' your head off for the last while.

HESTER. You've a nerve singin' that song. That song is mine! She made it for me and only me. Can't yees lave me with anythin'!

JOSEPH. I didn't know it was yours. She used sing it to me all the time.

HESTER. You're lyin'! Faithless! All of yees! Faithless! If she showed up now I'd spit in her face, I'd box the jaws off of her, I'd go after her with a knife, I'd make her squeal like a cornered badger. Where is she? She said she'd return. I've waited so long. I've waited so long — Have you come across her where you are?

JOSEPH. Death's a big country, Hester. She could be anywhere in it.

HESTER. No, she's alive. I can smell her. She's comin' towards me. I know it. Why doesn't she come and be done with it! If ya see her tell her I won't be hard on her, will ya?

JOSEPH. Aye, if I see her.

HESTER. Tell her there's just a couple of things I need to ax her, will ya?

JOSEPH. I will.

HESTER. I just want to know why, that's all.

JOSEPH. Why what?

HESTER. Was it somethin' I done on her? I was seven, same as me daughter Josie, seven, and there isn't anythin' in this wide world Josie could do that'd make me walk away from her.

JOSEPH. Ya have a daughter?

HESTER. Aye, they're tryin' to take her from me. Just let them try!

JOSEPH. Who's tryin'?

HESTER. If it wasn't for you, me and Carthage'd still be together!

JOSEPH. So it's my fault ya killed me, that what you're sayin'?

HESTER. He took your money after we killed ya —

JOSEPH. To my memory Carthage did nothin' only look on. I think he was as shocked as I was when ya came at me with the fishin' knife —

HESTER. He took your money! He helped me throw ya overboard! And now he wants to put it all on me.

JOSEPH. Ya came at me from behind, didn't ya? Wan minute I'm rowin' and the next I'm a ghost.

HESTER. If ya hadn't been such an arrogant git I may have left ya alone but ya just wouldn't shut up talkin' about her as if she wasn't my mother at all. The big smug neck of ya! It was axin' to be cut. And she even called ya after her. And calls me Hester. What sourt of a name is Hester? Hester's after no wan. And she saves her own name for you — Didn't she ever tell ya about me?

JOSEPH. She never mentioned ya.

HESTER. She must've. It's a long time ago. Think, will ya. Didn't she ever say anythin' about me?

JOSEPH. Only what she tould me father. She never spoke to me about ya.

HESTER. Listen to ya! You're still goin' on as if she was yours and you only an auld ghost! You're still talkin' as if I never existed.

JOSEPH. I don't know what you're on about, Hester, but if it's any consolation to ya, she left me too and our father. Josie Swane hung around for no wan.

HESTER. What age were ya when she left ya?

JOSEPH. Goin' on ten.

HESTER. Goin' on ten — that's three year more ya had of her than me — and me all that time waitin' for her and her all the time molly cuddlin' you — What was she like, Joseph? Every day I forget more and more till I'm startin' to think I made her up out of the air. If it wasn't for this auld caravan I'd swear I only dreamt her. What was she like?

JOSEPH. Well, she was big for starters.

HESTER. Aye, a big rancorous hulk.

JOSEPH. And she was fierce silent — gentle I suppose in her way.

HESTER. Gentle! She'd a vicious whiskey temper on her and a whiplash tongue and fists that'd land on ya like lightnin'.

JOSEPH. She never laid a hand on me — though I remember her fightin' with me father alright. He wasn't able for her at all. He'd be skulkin' round the house and her blowin' off about somethin' or other and her twice the size of him. I remember her goin' after him with a brush wan time. "What're ya at?" says he and he backin' away from her. "I'm spring cleanin'," says she and she sweepin' him out the door — It wasn't his fault, Hester, she told

46

him you were dead, that ya died at birth, it wasn't his fault. Ya would've liked the old man, but she told him ya died, that ya were born with your heart all wrong.

HESTER. Nothin' wrong of me heart till she set about banjaxin' it. The lyin' tongue of her. And he just believed her.

JOSEPH. Didn't he send me lookin' for ya in the end, see was there any trace of ya, told me to split the money with ya if I found ya. Hester, I was goin' to split the money with ya. I had it there in the boat. I was goin' to split it with ya when we reached the shore, ya didn't have to cut me throat for it.

HESTER. Ya think I slit your throat for a few auld pound me father left me?

JOSEPH. Then why?

HESTER. She stole my life from me.

JOSEPH. So you stole mine.

HESTER. Well somewan had to pay.

JOSEPH. If ya knew what it was like here ya'd never have done what ya done.

HESTER. Oh I think I know, Joseph, and I this year's an apprentice ghost.

JOSEPH. I'll be off, Hester, I didn't come for a row, I just wanted to say hello.

HESTER. Where are ya goin'?

JOSEPH. Just stravagin' the shadows.

HESTER. Look out for me over there.

JOSEPH. It's not wan bit romantic bein' dead, let me tell ya.

HESTER. I never thought it was. (*And exit Joseph. Hester sits on the steps of the caravan, drinks some wine from the bottle she took from the wedding, lights a cigar. Monica shouts offstage.*)

MONICA. Hester! Hester! Your house! It's on fire! Hester! (*Runs on.*) Come quick, I'll get the others!

HESTER. Don't bother.

MONICA. But your house — Ya set it yourself?

HESTER. I did.

MONICA. Christ almighty woman, are ya gone mad!

HESTER. Ya want a drink?

MONICA. A drink, she says! I better go and get Carthage, the livestock, the calves —

47

HESTER. Would ya calm down, Monica, only an auld house, it should never have been built in the first place. Let the bog have it back. In a year or so, it'll be covered in gorse and furze, a tree'll grow out through the roof, maybe a big bog oak. I never liked that house anyway.

MONICA. That's what the tinkers do, isn't it, burn everythin' after them?

HESTER. Aye.

MONICA. They'll skin ya alive, Hester, I'm tellin' ya, they'll kill ya.

HESTER. And you with them.

MONICA. I stood up for ya as best I could, I've to live round here, Hester. I had to pay me respects to the Cassidys. Sure Xavier and meself used walk to school together.

HESTER. Wan of these days you'll die of niceness, Monica Murray.

MONICA. A quality you've never had any time for.

HESTER. I'm just wan big lump of maneness and bad thoughts. Sit down, have a drink with me, I'll get ya a glass. *(Goes into the caravan, gets one.)* Sit down before ya fall.

MONICA. *(Sitting on steps, tipsily.)* We'll go off in this yoke, you and me.

HESTER. Will we?

MONICA. Flee off from this place, flee off to Eden.

HESTER. Eden — I left Eden, Monica, at the age of seven. It was on account of a look be this caravan at dusk. A look from a pair of nonchalant eyes, the colour of which I'm still not sure of.

MONICA. And who was it gave ya this look, your mother, was it? Josie Swane?

HESTER. Oh aye, Monica, she was the wan alright who looked at me so askance and strangely — Who'd believe a look could destroy ya? I never would've 'cept it happened to me.

MONICA. She was a harsh auld yoke, Hester, came and went like the moon. Ya'd wake wan mornin' and look out over the bog and ya'd see a fire and know she had returned. And I'd bring her down a sup of milk or a few eggs and she'd be here sittin' on the step just like you are, with her big head of black hair and eyes glamin' like a cat and long arms and a powerful neck all knotted that she'd stretch like a swan in a yawn and me with ne'er a neck at all. But

I was never comfortable with her, riddled by her, though, and I wasn't the only wan. There was lots spent evenin's tryin' to figure Josie Swane, somethin' cold and dead about her except when she sang and then I declare ya'd fall in love with her.

HESTER. Would ya now?

MONICA. There was a time round here when no celebration was complete without Josie Swane. She'd be invited everywhere to sing, funerals, weddin's, christenin's, birthdays of the bigger farmers, the harvest. And she'd make up songs for each occasion. And it wasn't so much they wanted her there, more they were afraid not to have her.

HESTER. I used go with her on some of them singin' sprees before she ran off. And she'd make up the song as we walked to wherever we were goin'. Sometimes she'd sing somethin' completely different than the song she'd been makin' on the road. Them were her "Blast from God" songs as opposed to her "Workaday" songs, or so she called them. And they never axed us to stay, these people, to sit down and ate with them, just lapped up her songs, gave her a bag of food and a half a crown and walked us off the premises, for fear we'd steal somethin', I suppose. I don't think it bothered her, it did me — and still rankles after all these years. But not Josie Swane, she'd be off to the shop to buy cigars and beer and sweets for me.

MONICA. Is there another sup of wine there? ·

HESTER. (Pours for her.) I'm all the time wonderin' whatever happened to her.

MONICA. You're still waitin' on her, aren't ya?

HESTER. This thirty-three years and it's still like she only walked away yesterday.

MONICA. She's not comin' back, Hester. I know what it's like to wait for somewan who's never walkin' through the door again. But this waitin' is only a fancy of yours. Now I don't make out to know anythin' about the workin's of this world but I know this much, it don't yield aisy to mortal wishes. And maybe that's the way it has to be. You up on forty, Hester, and still dreamin' of storybook endin's, still whingin' for your Mam.

HESTER. I made a promise, Monica, a promise to meself a long while back, all them years I was in the Industrial school I swore to meself that wan day I'm comin' back to the Bog of Cats to wait for her there and I'm never lavin' again.

MONICA. Well, I don't know how ya'll swing to stay now, your house in ashes, ya after appearin' in that dress. They're sayin' it's a black art thing ya picked up somewhere.

HESTER. A black art thing. *(Laughs.)* If I knew any black art things, by Christ, I'd use them now. The only way I'm lavin' this place is in a box and if it comes to that I'm not lavin' alone. I'll take yees all with me. And, yes, there's things about me yees never understood and makes yees afraid and yees are right for other things goes through my veins besides blood that I've fought so hard to keep wraps on.

MONICA. And what things are they?

HESTER. I don't understand them meself.

MONICA. Stop this wild talk then, I don't like it.

HESTER. Carthage still at the weddin'?

MONICA. And where else would he be?

HESTER. And what sourt of mood is he in?

MONICA. I wasn't mindin'. Don't waste your time over a man like him, faithless as an acorn on a high wind — wine all gone?

HESTER. Aye.

MONICA. I'll go up to the feast and bring us back a bottle unless you've any objections.

HESTER. I'll drink the enemy's wine. Not the wine's fault it fell into the paws of cutthroats and gargiyles.

MONICA. Be back in a while, so.

HESTER. And check see Josie's alright, will ya?

MONICA. She's dancin' her little heart out. *(Exit Monica. Hester looks around, up at the winter sky of stars, shivers.)*

HESTER. Well, it's dusk now and long after and where are ya, Mr. Ghost Fancier. I'm here waitin' for ya, though I've been tould to flee. Maybe you're not comin' after all, maybe I only imagined ya. *(Enter Josie running, excited.)*

JOSIE. Mam! — Mam! I'm goin' on the honeymoon with Daddy and Caroline.

HESTER. You're goin' no such where.

JOSIE. Ah, Mam, they're goin' drivin' to the sea. I never seen the sea.

HESTER. It's just wan big bog hole, Josie, and blue, that's all, nothin' remarkable about it.

JOSIE. Well, Daddy says I'm goin'.

HESTER. Don't mind your Daddy.

JOSIE. No, I want to go with them. It's only for five days, Mam.

HESTER. There's a couple of things you should know about your precious Daddy, ya should know how he has treated me!

JOSIE. I'm not listenin' to ya givin' out about him. *(Covers her ears with her hands.)*

HESTER. That's right, stand up for him and see how far it'll get ya. He swore to me that after you'd been born he'd marry me and now he plans to take ya off of me. I suppose ya'd like that too.

JOSIE. *(Still with ears covered.)* I said I'm not listenin'!

HESTER. *(Pulls Josie's hands from her ears.)* You'll listen to me, Josie Swane, and you listen well. Another that had your name walked away from me. Your perfect Daddy walked away from me. And you'll walk from me too. All me life people have walked away without a word of explanation. Well, I want to tell ya somethin', Josie, if you lave me ya'll die.

JOSIE. I will not.

HESTER. Ya will! Ya will! It's a sourt of curse was put on ya be the Catwoman and the black swan. Remember the black swan?

JOSIE. Aye. *(Frightened.)*

HESTER. So ya have to stay with me, d'ya see, and if your Daddy or anywan else axes ya who ya'd prefer to live with, ya have to say me.

JOSIE. Mam, I would've said you anyway.

HESTER. Would ya? — Oh, I'm sorry, Josie, I'm sorry, sweetheart. It's not true what I said about a curse bein' put on ya, it's not true at all. If I'm let go tonight I swear I'll make it up to ya for them awful things I'm after sayin'.

JOSIE. It's alright, Mam, I know ya didn't mean it — Can I go back to the weddin'? The dancin's not over yet.

HESTER. Dance with me. *(Begins waltzing with Josie, music.)* Come on, we'll have our own weddin'. *(Picks her up, they swirl and twirl to the music.)* Ya beautiful, beautiful child, I could ate ya.

JOSIE. I could ate ya too — Can I go back to the weddin' for a while?

HESTER. Ya can do anythin' ya want 'cept lave me. *(Puts her down.)* G'wan then, for half an hour.

51

JOSIE. I brung ya a big lump of weddin' cake in me handbag. Here. Why wasn't it your weddin', Mam?

HESTER. It sourt of was. G'wan and enjoy yourself. (*And exit Josie running. Hester looks after her eating the wedding cake. Xavier Cassidy comes up behind her from the shadows, demonic, red-faced, drink taken, carries a gun.*)

XAVIER. Ya enjoyin' that, are ya, Swane, me daughter's weddin' cake?

HESTER. Oh it's yourself, Xavier, with your auld gun. I was wonderin' when I'd see ya in your true colours. Must've been an awful strain on ya behavin' so well all day.

XAVIER. Ya burnt the bloody house to the ground.

HESTER. Did ya really think I was goin' to have your daughter livin' there?

XAVIER. Ya won't best me, Swane, ya know that. I ran your mother out of here and I'll run you too like a frightened hare.

HESTER. It's got nothin' to do with ya, Cassidy, it's between me and Carthage.

XAVIER. Got everythin' to do with me and ya after makin' a mockery of me and me daughter in front of the whole parish.

HESTER. No more than yees deserve for wheedlin' and cajolin' Carthage away from me with your promises of land and money.

XAVIER. He was aisy wheedled.

HESTER. He was always a feckless fool.

XAVIER. Aye, in all respects bar wan. He loves the land and like me he'd rather die than part with it wance he gets his greedy hands on it. With him Cassidy's farm'll be safe, the name'll be gone, but never the farm. And who's to say but maybe your little bastard and her offspring won't be farmin' my land in years to come.

HESTER. Josie'll have nothin' to do with anythin' that's yours. I'll see to that. And if ya'd looked after your own son better ya wouldn't be covetin' Josie nor any that belongs to me.

XAVIER. Don't you talk about my young fella.

HESTER. Wasn't it me that found him, strychnined to the eye-balls, howlin' 'long the bog and his dog in his arms?

XAVIER. How was I supposed to know he'd go and dig the dog up?

HESTER. You're not a farmer for nothin', somethin' about that young lad bothered ya, he wasn't tough enough for ya probably, so ya strychnined his dog, knowin' full well the child'd be goin' lookin' for him. And ya know what strychnine does, a tayspoonfull is all it takes, and ya'd the dog showered in it. Burnt his hands clean away. Ya knew what ya were at, Cassidy, and ya know I know. I can tell the darkness in you, ya know how? Because it mirrors me own. And that's why ya want me out of here. And maybe you're right. I can't tell anymore.

XAVIER. Fabrications! Fabrications of a mind unhinged! My son died in a tragic accident of no wan's makin'. That's what the inquest said. My conscience is clear.

HESTER. Is it now? Well, I don't believe in tragic accidents and especially not where you're concerned.

XAVIER. If ya could just hear the mad talk of yourself, Swane, and the cut of ya. You're mad as your mother and she was a lunatic.

HESTER. Nothin' lunatic about her 'cept she couldn't breathe the same air as yees all here by the Bog of Cats.

XAVIER. We often breathed the same air, me and Josie Swane, she was a loose wan, loose and lazy and aisy, a five shillin' hoor, like you.

HESTER. If you're tryin' to destroy some high idea I have of her you're wastin' your time. I've spent long hours of all the long years thinkin' about her. There isn't a situation I haven't imagined her in. I've lived through every mood there is to live concernin' her. Sure there was a time I hated her and wished the worst for her, but I've taught meself to rise above all that is cruel and unworthy in me thinkin' about her. So don't you think your five shillin' hoor stories will ever change me opinion of her. I have memories your cheap talk can never alter.

XAVIER. And what memories are they, Swane? I'd like to know if they exist at all.

HESTER. Oh they exist alright and ya'd like to rob them from me along with everythin' else. But ya won't because I'm stronger than ya and ya'll take nothin' from me I don't choose to give ya.

XAVIER. (Puts gun to her throat.) Won't I now? Think ya'll outwit me with your tinker ways and —

HESTER. Let go of me!

XAVIER. (A tighter grip.) Now let's see the leftovers of Carthage Kilbride. (Uses gun to look down her dress.)

HESTER. I'm warnin' ya, let go! (A struggle, a few blows, he wins *this bout.)*

XAVIER. Now are ya stronger than me? I could do what I wanted with ya right here and now and no wan would believe ya. Now what I'd really like to know is when are ya plannin' on lavin'?

HESTER. What're ya goin' to do, Cassidy? Blow me head off?

XAVIER. I married me daughter today, now I don't care for the whiny little rip that much, but she's all I've got, and I don't want Carthage changin' his mind after a while. So when are ya lavin', Swane? When?

HESTER. Ya think I'm afraid of you and your auld gun. *(Puts her mouth over the barrel.)* G'wan shoot! Blow me away! Save me the bother meself. *(Goes for the trigger.)* Ya want me to do it for ya? *(Another struggle, this time Xavier trying to get away from her.)*

XAVIER. You're a dangerous witch, Swane.

HESTER. *(Laughs at him.)* You're sweatin'. Always knew ya were yella to the bone. Don't worry, I'll be lavin' this place tonight, though not the way you or anywan else expects. Ya call me a witch, Cassidy? This is nothin', you just wait and see the real — *(Enter Carthage running, enraged, shakes her violently.)*

CARTHAGE. The cattle! The calves! Ya burnt them all, they're roarin' in the flames! The house in ashes! A'ya gone mad altogether! The calves! A'ya gone mad!

HESTER. *(Shakes him off.)* No, I only meant what I said. I warned ya, Carthage, ya drove me to it.

XAVIER. A hundred year ago we'd strap ya to a stake and roast ya till your guts exploded.

CARTHAGE. That's it! I'm takin' Josie off of ya! I don't care if I've to drag ya through the courts. I'll have ya put away! I'll tell all about your brother! I don't care!

HESTER. Tell them! And tell them your own part in it too while you're at it! Don't you threaten me with Josie! This pervert has just been gropin' me with his gun and you want Josie round him —

XAVIER. The filthy lies of her —

HESTER. Bringin' a child on a honeymoon, what are ya at, Carthage? Well, I won't let ya use Josie to fill in the silences between yourself and Caroline Cassidy —

XAVIER. She's beyond reasonin' with, if she was mine I'd cut that tinker tongue from her mouth, I'd brand her lips, I'd —

CARTHAGE. *(Exploding at Xavier.)* Would you just go back to the weddin' and lave us alone, stop interferin'. If ya'd only let me handle it all the way I wanted to, but, no, ya had to push and bring the weddin' forward to avoid your taxes, just lave us alone, will ya!

XAVIER. I will and gladly. You're a fiasco, Kilbride, like all the Kilbrides before ya, ya can't control a mere woman, ya'll control nothin', I'm havin' serious doubts about signin' over me farm —

CARTHAGE. Keep your bloody farm, Cassidy. I have me own. I'm not your scrubber boy. There's other things besides land.

XAVIER. There's nothin' besides land, boy, nothin', and a real farmer would never think otherwise.

CARTHAGE. Just go back to the weddin', I'll follow ya in a while and we can try hammerin' out our differences.

XAVIER. Can we? *(Exit Xavier.)*

HESTER. All's not well in Paradise.

CARTHAGE. All'd be fine if I could do away with you.

HESTER. If ya just let me stay I'll cause no more trouble. I'll move into the caravan with Josie. In time ya may be glad to have me around. I've been your greatest friend around here, Carthage, doesn't that count for nothin' now?

CARTHAGE. I'm not havin' me daughter livin' in a caravan!

HESTER. There was a time you loved this caravan.

CARTHAGE. Will ya just stop tryin' to drag up them years! It won't work!

HESTER. Ya promised me things! Ya built that house for me. Ya wanted me to see how normal people lived. And I went along with ya again' me better judgement. All I ever wanted was to be by the Bog of Cats. A modest want when compared with the wants of others. Just let me stay here in the caravan.

CARTHAGE. And have the whole neighbourhood makin' a laughin' stock of me?

HESTER. That's not why ya won't let me stay. You're ashamed of your part in me brother's death, aren't ya?

CARTHAGE. I had no part in it!

HESTER. You're afraid I'll tell everywan what ya done. I won't. I wouldn't ever, Carthage.

CARTHAGE. I done nothin' except watch!

HESTER. Ya helped me tie a stone around his waist!

CARTHAGE. He was dead by then!

HESTER. He wasn't! His pulse was still goin'!

CARTHAGE. You're only sayin' that now to torture me! Why did ya do it, Hetty? We were doin' fine till then.

HESTER. Somethin' evil moved in me blood — and the fishin' knife was there in the bottom of the boat — and Bergit's Lake was wide — and I looked across the lake to me father's house and it went through me like a spear that she had a whole other life there — How could she have and I a part of her?

CARTHAGE. Ya never said any of this before — I always thought ya killed your brother for the money.

HESTER. I met his ghost tonight, ya know —

CARTHAGE. His ghost?

HESTER. Aye, a gentle ghost and so lost, and he spoke so softly to me, I didn't deserve such softness —

CARTHAGE. Ah, would you stop this talk!

HESTER. You rose in the world on his ashes! And that's what haunts ya and that's why ya want to forget I ever existed. Well, I won't let ya. You'll remember me, Carthage, when the dust settles, when ya grow tired scourin' acres and bank balances. Ya'll remember me when ya walk them big empty childless rooms in Cassidy's house. Ya think now ya won't, but ya will.

CARTHAGE. Ya always had a high opinion of yourself. Aye, I'll remember ya from time to time. I'll remember ya sittin' at the kitchen table drinkin' till all hours and I'll remember the sound of the back door closin' as ya escaped for another night roamin' the bog.

HESTER. The drinkin' came after, long after you put it into your mind to lave me. If I had somewan to talk to I mightn't have drunk so hard, somewan to roam the bog with me, somewan to take away a tiny piece of this guilt I carry with me, but ya never would.

CARTHAGE. Seems I done nothin' right. Did I not?

HESTER. You want to glane lessons for your new bride. No, Carthage, ya done nothin' right, your bull-headed pride and economy and painful advancement never moved me. What I wanted was somewan to look me in the eye and know I was understood and not judged. You thought I had no right to ax for that. Maybe

I hadn't, but the way ya used to judge me — didn't it ever occur to ya, that however harshly ya judged me, I judged meself harsher. Couldn't ya ever see that.

CARTHAGE. I'm takin' Josie, Hester. I'm takin' her off of ya. It's plain as day to everywan 'cept yourself ya can't look after her. If you're wise ya'll lave it at that and not take us muckin' through the courts. I'll let ya see her from time to time.

HESTER. Take her then, take her, ya've taken everythin' else. In me stupidity I thought ya'd lave me Josie. I should've known ya always meant to take her too. *(Enter Caroline with a bottle of wine.)*

CAROLINE. *(To Carthage.)* Oh, this is where ya are.

CARTHAGE. She's after burnin' all the livestock, the house, the sheds in ruins. I'm away up there now to see what can be salvaged. G'wan back home, I'll be there in a while. *(And exit Carthage.)*

CAROLINE. Monica said ya wanted wine, I opened it for ya.

HESTER. Take more than wine to free me from this place. Take some kind of dark sprung miracle. *(Takes the wine.)*

CARTHAGE. *(Coming back.)* Caroline, come on, come on, I don't want ya around her.

HESTER. G'wan back to your weddin' like Carthage says. *(Caroline goes to exit, stops.)*

CAROLINE. I just wanted to say —

HESTER. What? Ya just wanted to say what?

CAROLINE. Nothin' — Only I'll be very good to Josie whenev- · er she stays with us.

HESTER. Will ya now?

CAROLINE. I won't let her out of me sight — I'll go everywhere with her — protect her from things — That's all. *(Goes to exit.)*

HESTER. Didn't ya enjoy your big weddin' day, Caroline?

CAROLINE. No, I didn't — Everywan too loud and frantic — and when ya turned up in that weddin' dress, knew it should've been you — and Daddy drinkin' too much and shoutin', and Carthage gone away in himself, just watchin' it all like it had nothin' to do with him, and everywan laughin' behind me back and pityin' me — When me mother was alive, I used go into the sick room to talk to her and she used take me into the bed beside her and she'd describe for me me weddin' day. Of how she'd be there with a big hat on her and so proud. And the weddin' was goin' to

57

be in this big ballroom with a fountain of mermaids in the middle, instead of Daddy's idea of havin' the do at home like his own weddin' — None of it was how it was meant to be, none of it.

HESTER. Nothin' ever is, Caroline. Nothin'. I've been a long time wishin' over me mother too. For too long now I've imagined her comin' towards me across the Bog of Cats and she would find me here standin' strong. She would see me life was complete, that I had Carthage and Josie and me own house. I so much wanted her to see that I had flourished without her and maybe then I could forgive her — Caroline, he's takin' Josie from me.

CAROLINE. He's not, he wouldn't do that, Hester.

HESTER. He's just been here tellin' me.

CAROLINE. I won't let him, I'll talk to him, I'll stand up for ya on that account.

HESTER. Ya never stood up for nothin' yet, I doubt ya'll stand up for me. Anyway, they won't listen to ya. You're only a little china bit of a girl. I could break ya aisy as a tay cup or a wine glass. But I won't. Ya know why? Because I knew ya when ya were Josie's age, a scrawky little thing that hung on the scraps of my affection. Anyway, no need to break ya, you were broke a long while back.

CAROLINE. I wanted to be a kindergarten teacher or a air hostess or a beautician. *(Stands there, lost-looking.)*

HESTER. G'wan back to your weddin' and lave me be.

CAROLINE. I promise ya I'll do everythin' I can about Josie.

HESTER. *(Softly.)* G'wan. G'wan. *(Exit Caroline, Hester stands there alone, takes a drink, goes into the caravan, comes out with a knife. She tests it for sharpness, teases it across her throat, shivers.)* Come on, ya done it aisy enough to another, now it's your own turn. *(Bares her throat, ready to do it. Enter Josie running, stops, sees Hester with the knife poised.)*

JOSIE. Mam — What's that ya've got there?

HESTER. *(Stops.)* Just an auld fishin' knife, Josie, I've had this years.

JOSIE. And what are ya doin' with it?

HESTER. Nothin', Josie, nothin'.

JOSIE. I came to say goodbye, we'll be goin' soon. *(Kisses Hester.)*

HESTER. Goodbye, sweetheart — Josie, ya won't see me again now.

JOSIE. I will so. I'm only goin' on a honeymoon.

HESTER. No, Josie, ya won't see me again because I'm goin' away too.

JOSIE. Where?

HESTER. Somewhere ya can never return from.

JOSIE. And where's that?

HESTER. Never mind. I only wanted to tell ya goodbye, that's all.

JOSIE. Well, can I go with ya?

HESTER. No, ya can't.

JOSIE. Ah, Mam, I want to be where you'll be.

HESTER. Well, ya can't, because wance ya go there ya can never come back.

JOSIE. I wouldn't want to if you're not here, Mam.

HESTER. You're just bein' contrary now. Don't ya want to be with your Daddy and grow up big and lovely and full of advantages they tell me I have not the power to give ya.

JOSIE. Mam, I'd be watchin' for ya all the time 'long the Bog of Cats. I'd be hopin' and waitin' and prayin' for ya to return.

HESTER. Don't be sayin' those things to me now.

JOSIE. Just take me with ya, Mam. *(Puts her arms around Hester.)*

HESTER. No, ya don't understand. Go away, get away from me, g'wan now, run away from me quickly now.

JOSIE. *(Struggling to stay in contact with Hester.)* No, Mam, stop! I'm goin' with ya!

HESTER. Would ya let go!

JOSIE. *(Frantic.)* No, Mam. Please!

HESTER. Alright, alright! Shhh! *(Picks her up.)* It's alright, I'll take ya with me, I won't have ya as I was, waitin' a lifetime for somewan to return, because they don't, Josie, they don't. It's alright. Close your eyes. *(Josie closes her eyes.)* Are they closed tight?

JOSIE. Yeah. *(Hester cuts Josie's throat in one savage movement.)*

JOSIE. *(Softly.)* Mam — Mam — *(And Josie dies in her arms.)*

HESTER. *(Whispers.)* It's because ya wanted to come, Josie. *(Begins to wail. Enter the Catwoman.)*

CATWOMAN. Hester, what is it? What is it?

HESTER. Oh, Catwoman, I knew somethin' terrible'd happen, I never thought it'd be this. *(Continues wailing.)*

CATWOMAN. What have ya done, Hester? Have ya harmed yourself?

HESTER. No, not meself and yes meself.

CATWOMAN. *(Comes over, feels around Hester, feels Josie.)* Not Josie, Hester? Not Josie? Lord on high, Hester, not the child. I thought yourself, maybe, or Carthage, but never the child. *(Runs to the edge of the stage shouting.)* Help, somewan, help! Hester Swane's after butcherin' the child! Help! *(Hester walks around demented with Josie. Enter Carthage running.)*

CARTHAGE. What is it, Catwoman? Hester? What's wrong with Josie? There's blood all over her.

HESTER. Lave off, you. Lave off. I warned ya and I tould ya, would ya listen, what've I done, what've I done? *(The others drift on in ones and twos.)*

CARTHAGE. Give her to me!

MONICA. Sweet Jesus, Hester —

CARTHAGE. Give her to me! Will somewan go and get some-wan. You've killed her, ya've killed her.

HESTER. Yees all thought I was just goin' to walk away and lave her at yeer mercy. I almost did. But she's mine and I wouldn't have her waste her life dreamin' about me and yees thwartin' her with black stories against me.

CARTHAGE. You're a savage! *(Enter the Ghost Fancier. Hester sees him, the others don't. He picks up the fishing knife.)*

HESTER. You're late, ya came too late.

CARTHAGE. What's she sayin'? What? Give her to me, come on now. *(Takes Josie off Hester.)*

HESTER. Ya won't forget me now, Carthage, and when all of this is over or half-remembered and ya think ya've almost forgotten me again, take a walk along the Bog of Cats and wait for a purlin' wind through your hair or a soft breath be your ear or a rustle behind ya. That'll be me and Josie ghostin' ya. *(She walks towards the Ghost Fancier.)* Take me away, take me away from here.

GHOST FANCIER. Alright, my lovely. *(They go into a death dance with the fishing knife, which ends plunged into Hester's heart. She falls; to the ground.)*

HESTER. *(Whispers as she dies.)* Mam — Mam — *(Monica goes over to her after a while.)*

MONICA. Hester — She's gone — Hester — She's cut her heart out — it's lyin' there on top of her chest like some dark feathered bird. *(Music. Lights. End.)*

End of Play

SONGS OF JOSIE SWANE *

BY THE BOG OF CATS

By the Bog of Cats I finally learned false from true,
Learned too late that it was you and only you
Left me sore, a heart brimfull of rue
By the Bog of Cats in the darkling dew.

By the Bog of Cats I dreamed a dream of wooing.
I heard your clear voice to me a-calling
That I must go though it be my undoing.
By the Bog of Cats I'll stay no more a-rueing.

To the Bog of Cats I one day will return,
In mortal form or in ghostly form,
And I will find you there and there with you sojourn,
Forever by the Bog of Cats, my darling one.

THE BLACK SWAN

I know where a black swan sleeps
On the bank of grey water,
Hidden in a nest of leaves
So none can disturb her.

I have lain outside her lair,
My hand upon her wing,
And I have whispered to her
And of my sorrows sung.

I wish I was a black swan
And could fly away from here,
But I am Josie Swane,
Without wings, without care.

* *To be recorded and used during the play.*

NEW PLAYS

★ **AT HOME AT THE ZOO by Edward Albee.** Edward Albee delves deeper into his play THE ZOO STORY by adding a first act, HOMELIFE, which precedes Peter's fateful meeting with Jerry on a park bench in Central Park. "An essential and heartening experience." *–NY Times.* "Darkly comic and thrilling." *–Time Out.* "Genuinely fascinating." *–Journal News.* [2M, 1W] ISBN: 978-0-8222-2317-7

★ **PASSING STRANGE book and lyrics by Stew, music by Stew and Heidi Rodewald, created in collaboration with Annie Dorsen.** A daring musical about a young bohemian that takes you from black middle-class America to Amsterdam, Berlin and beyond on a journey towards personal and artistic authenticity. "Fresh, exuberant, bracingly inventive, bitingly funny, and full of heart." *–NY Times.* "The freshest musical in town!" *–Wall Street Journal.* "Excellent songs and a vulnerable heart." *–Variety.* [4M, 3W] ISBN: 978-0-8222-2400-6

★ **REASONS TO BE PRETTY by Neil LaBute.** Greg really, truly adores his girlfriend, Steph. Unfortunately, he also thinks she has a few physical imperfections, and when he mentions them, all hell breaks loose. "Tight, tense and emotionally true." *–Time Magazine.* "Lively and compulsively watchable." *–The Record.* [2M, 2W] ISBN: 978-0-8222-2394-8

★ **OPUS by Michael Hollinger.** With only a few days to rehearse a grueling Beethoven masterpiece, a world-class string quartet struggles to prepare their highest-profile performance ever—a televised ceremony at the White House. "Intimate, intense and profoundly moving." *–Time Out.* "Worthy of scores of bravissimos." *–BroadwayWorld.com.* [4M, 1W] ISBN: 978-0-8222-2363-4

★ **BECKY SHAW by Gina Gionfriddo.** When an evening calculated to bring happiness takes a dark turn, crisis and comedy ensue in this wickedly funny play that asks what we owe the people we love and the strangers who land on our doorstep. "As engrossing as it is ferociously funny." *–NY Times.* "Gionfriddo is some kind of genius." *–Variety.* [2M, 3W] ISBN: 978-0-8222-2402-0

★ **KICKING A DEAD HORSE by Sam Shepard.** Hobart Struther's horse has just dropped dead. In an eighty-minute monologue, he discusses what path brought him here in the first place, the fate of his marriage, his career, politics and eventually the nature of the universe. "Deeply instinctual and intuitive." *–NY Times.* "The brilliance is in the infinite reverberations Shepard extracts from his simple metaphor." *–TheaterMania.* [1M, 1W] ISBN: 978-0-8222-2336-8

DRAMATISTS PLAY SERVICE, INC.
440 Park Avenue South, New York, NY 10016 212-683-8960 Fax 212-213-1539
postmaster@dramatists.com www.dramatists.com

NEW PLAYS

★ **AUGUST: OSAGE COUNTY by Tracy Letts.** WINNER OF THE 2008 PULITZER PRIZE AND TONY AWARD. When the large Weston family reunites after Dad disappears, their Oklahoma homestead explodes in a maelstrom of repressed truths and unsettling secrets. "Fiercely funny and bitingly sad." *–NY Times.* "Ferociously entertaining." *–Variety.* "A hugely ambitious, highly combustible saga." *–NY Daily News.* [6M, 7W] ISBN: 978-0-8222-2300-9

★ **RUINED by Lynn Nottage.** WINNER OF THE 2009 PULITZER PRIZE. Set in a small mining town in Democratic Republic of Congo, RUINED is a haunting, probing work about the resilience of the human spirit during times of war. "A full-immersion drama of shocking complexity and moral ambiguity." *–Variety.* "Sincere, passionate, courageous." *–Chicago Tribune.* [8M, 4W] ISBN: 978-0-8222-2390-0

★ **GOD OF CARNAGE by Yasmina Reza, translated by Christopher Hampton.** WINNER OF THE 2009 TONY AWARD. A playground altercation between boys brings together their Brooklyn parents, leaving the couples in tatters as the rum flows and tensions explode. "Satisfyingly primitive entertainment." *–NY Times.* "Elegant, acerbic, entertainingly fueled on pure bile." *–Variety.* [2M, 2W] ISBN: 978-0-8222-2399-3

★ **THE SEAFARER by Conor McPherson.** Sharky has returned to Dublin to look after his irascible, aging brother. Old drinking buddies Ivan and Nicky are holed up at the house too, hoping to play some cards. But with the arrival of a stranger from the distant past, the stakes are raised ever higher. "Dark and enthralling Christmas fable." *–NY Times.* "A timeless classic." *–Hollywood Reporter.* [5M] ISBN: 978-0-8222-2284-2

★ **THE NEW CENTURY by Paul Rudnick.** When the playwright is Paul Rudnick, expectations are geared for a play both hilarious and smart, and this provocative and outrageous comedy is no exception. "The one-liners fly like rockets." *–NY Times.* "The funniest playwright around." *–Journal News.* [2M, 3W] ISBN: 978-0-8222-2315-3

★ **SHIPWRECKED! AN ENTERTAINMENT—THE AMAZING ADVENTURES OF LOUIS DE ROUGEMONT (AS TOLD BY HIMSELF) by Donald Margulies.** The amazing story of bravery, survival and celebrity that left nineteenth-century England spellbound. Dare to be whisked away. "A deft, literate narrative." *–LA Times.* "Springs to life like a theatrical pop-up book." *–NY Times.* [2M, 1W] ISBN: 978-0-8222-2341-2

DRAMATISTS PLAY SERVICE, INC.
440 Park Avenue South, New York, NY 10016   212-683-8960   Fax 212-213-1539
postmaster@dramatists.com   www.dramatists.com